ORIGIN and DEVELOPMENT

of

NORTHEASTERN UNIVERSITY

1898 - 1960

by Everett C. Marston

Professor of English
Northeastern University

Published by Northeastern University, Boston, Massachusetts

Manufactured in the United States by The Cuneo Press of New England, Inc.

Copyright Northeastern University 1961

PREFACE

The purpose of this book is to report the history of Northeastern University, not in the form of a definitive factual record but as the story of an unusual institution of learning.

The time span of the history is not extensive—1896 to 1960—yet within that period a simple program of evening education for employed young men, conducted by the Boston Young Men's Christian Association, became a large and impressive university.

The assembling of this report has been difficult for two reasons. From 1898 until the years following World War I, the builders of Northeastern were unaware that they were developing a university; as a result, they did not record and preserve the information and interpretation which now would be of great value. The immediacy of time imposes the second handicap, since in 1960 an objective view of many events and people important to the history of Northeastern is impossible to establish. No doubt another recorder in 2060 will see these elements in authentic historical perspective.

The present story of Northeastern is the result of composite efforts. Although any errors of fact or sins of judgment must be the responsibility of the writer, many other people contributed, directly or indirectly, to the content of this book.

The setting and background of the Northeastern story was drawn from the writers listed in the Bibliography. The Annual Reports of the Boston Young Men's Christian Association from 1883 onward were a vital source of information, as were numerous University reports and records.

Dr. Carl Ell authorized this project in the fall of 1958, and in the following months provided invaluable data and general assistance.

A reviewing committee made up of Dr. Ell, Dr. William White, Dean Kenneth Ryder, and Mr. George Speers read first drafts of chapters and made corrections and suggestions.

Professors Joseph Spear, Harold Melvin, and Edward Parsons were helpful in many ways but particularly by evaluating the first version of the development of student activities at Northeastern.

Similarly, Dean Roy Wooldridge and Professors John Morgan and Thomas McMahon passed judgment on the chapter on Co-operative Education at Northeastern.

Mrs. Marjorie Prout contributed valuable information from memory, from extensive records which she had built up through past years, and in numerous folders labeled "Odds and Ends of NU History."

President Asa Knowles provided valuable assistance and made possible the final form of this history.

Mr. Landon Herrick of the Library staff, in charge of Archives, was helpful and co-operative; he performed a service for the University by systematizing a mass of historical material which earlier had been only a mass.

Miss Manola Simpson typed the first version of the manuscript and Virginia Ryder, an expert though volunteer worker, prepared the final version; both exercised editorial judgment as well as technical skill.

In addition, the following people contributed to the content of this book, in some instances without knowing they were doing so—Julian Jackson, Major Charles Skinner, Roland Moody, Frederick Holmes, William Wilkinson, Charles Havice, G. Raymond Fennell, Donald MacKenzie, Martin Essigmann, Richard Sprague, Robert Bruce, Loring Thompson, Rudolf Oberg, Milton Schlagenhauf, Charles Kitchin, William Miernyk, Galen Light, Emil Gramstorff, Herbert Gallagher, George Mallion, Arthur Vernon, Lester Vander Werf, Alfred Ferretti, Chester Baker, Albert Everett, Ralph Troupe, Charles Baird, Carl Muckenhoupt, Mrs. Mildred Garfield, Wilfred Lake, Myron Spencer, J. Kenneth Stevenson, Roger Hamilton, Franklin Norvish, William Alexander.

If, by this combined effort but with final responsibility resting with the writer, the story of Northeastern to 1960 reflects a portion of the imagination, courage, and enterprise which made a university, the time and effort have been well spent.

CONTENTS

I

THE TIME AND THE SETTING

Boston in the 1890's was a city glorying in its past, reveling in the present, and with a new and different future pressing in upon it impatiently.

The past had been long and distinguished, not only studded with such stirring events as those at Faneuil Hall, the Common, Bunker Hill, and Dorchester Heights, but with a vigorous nineteenth century coming to a close.

Major events were occurring in various parts of the world during the last decade of the century. In Germany, Bismarck "the Iron Chancellor" died in 1898, leaving as a monument to his long life a unified Germany and a legacy of trouble for the future. In France, in the same year, Marie and Pierre Curie brought their experiments to the point of discovering and establishing radium as a new element. In England, Victoria was the symbol of an empire, Queen of Britain and Empress of India, with the Diamond Jubilee of 1897 celebrating and demonstrating the greatness of the empire. In Central America and in the orient, uneasy developments were forming and growing.

An unstable balance of power and the pressure of new forces resulted in the Spanish-American War of 1898, a minor conflict in contrast to later wars since the four months of hostilities cost a mere $250,000 and a total of 5000 American lives, most of the deaths the result of disease rather than battle casualty. Yet the war resulted in ownership or protection by the United States of Cuba, Puerto Rico, Guam, and the Philippine Islands. With the addition of Hawaii to its possessions, the United States assumed the new and difficult role of world power, in territory as well as in responsibility and leadership.

Boston was involved, both directly and indirectly, in all of these wide developments. At the same time, Boston was preoccupied with its own affairs, for the 1890's ended a century of local expansion, material progress, and modernization.

The physical city was growing. The pear-shaped peninsula of 783 acres which constituted colonial Boston would become by 1903 an area of 1829 acres. Mill Cove in the North End, roughly from Haymarket Square to Causeway Street, had been filled during the first quarter of the nineteenth century. Over a hundred acres had been added in East Cove, along the present Atlantic Avenue section. In the 1830's the South Cove Company had redeemed from tidewater fifty-five acres of land lying southward from South Station. The Back Bay tidewater area had been in process of filling and development for forty years, and was absorbing more and more of the overflow population, including some people from the already congested North End. The terrain of Boston was beginning to acquire the extent and aspect which in our time are so familiar.

Inventions and improvements, bringing to portions of the Boston population the niceties of life, were beginning to be taken for granted.

In 1848 the opening of the water supply from Lake Cochituate to the streets and houses of Boston had been the occasion for high rejoicing, with parades, orations, fireworks, a man-made geyser rising sixty to eighty feet in the Frog Pond, and a day of freedom for all school children of the city. The Railroad Celebration, three years later, when Boston was connected by rail with Canada, was a round of banquets, yacht races, and the entertainment of distinguished visitors, including President Millard Fillmore.

In following decades such marvels as the telephone, the Boston subway, and even the common use of bathtubs and iceboxes, were accepted without celebration, or even much surprise. America was a growing, progressive nation, and Boston was assumed to be in the front line of advance.

The phrase "Athens of America" was still applied to Boston and its kindred intellectual suburbs of Cambridge and Concord, though the label was less used as time passed. The influential giants Daniel Webster, Emerson, Longfellow, Hawthorne, Thoreau, and others of their generation had passed from the scene. The impression they had made still lingered, however, and other and different great men were taking their places. A representative of distinguished public service was Chief Justice Oliver Wendell Holmes, who in 1902 would join the Supreme Court. At Harvard, William James and George Santayana were only two of the powerful minds that were to influence thinking in America and in the world.

As a background to the outstanding figures in law, science, scholarship, and the arts, Bostonian culture was a pattern unique in American cities, with deep roots and long, steady growth.

Institutions and traditions familiar in our time were already well established in the 1890's. The Lowell Institute, for example, had been founded in 1840, and the fact that it met a crying need of the time is supported by the report that in the second year of the Institute the crowds applying for free lecture tickets at the Old Corner Bookstore congregated in such numbers and with such enthusiasm that they broke in the windows of the store. The Handel and Haydn Society, an outgrowth of the choral group of Park Street Church, was founded in 1815, and in later decades, along with the Academy of Music, visits by orchestras from abroad, the New England Conservatory of Music, and the Boston Symphony Orchestra, made Boston an impressive name in the world of music.

Added fame was coming to Boston from more recent and different institutions. One illustration is the Massachusetts Institute of Technology, which developed from the work of William Barton Rogers who in the 1860's came from the University of Virginia to launch in Boston a School of Industrial Science.

Although Boston might later cease to be called an Athens, with other connotations attaching to its name, in the 1890's it was a city of widespread intellectual and artistic activity and a cultural status accepted without question in America and in Europe.

Like almost any other decade in the long history of Boston, the period of the '90's was one of transition. Under the pressure of industrial growth and changing as well as growing population, the city was being forced in new directions.

The expansion of manufacture, following the long period of shipping and foreign trade, brought new wealth, new family fortunes, and in some segments of the population a higher standard of living, to Boston and to all of Massachusetts.

It also brought problems. In the pre-Civil War period, Boston Abolitionists found it easy and perhaps convenient to concentrate on the freeing of the slave, and to ignore or minimize the deterioration of public health and morals in such towns as Lawrence and Lowell, where cotton mills required and somehow found an increasing number of workers, including thousands of young women from rural New England and from foreign countries. After the Civil War, and especially after 1880, the industrial development of Massachusetts accelerated, and was paralleled by other developments which made for a changing population and attendant complexities.

Immigration from the Old World to New England had started in 1620. In the nineteenth century, however, America became the land of opportunity in a new sense. The famines in Ireland in 1846 and 1847 resulted in the beginning of an increasing stream of immigrants to New England, with Boston as a focal point. Among the later national groups, immigrants from Italy and Russia were most conspicuous in Boston; consequently, the population in sections of the city, notably the North End, changed in proportion and dominance as decades passed.

4

The Time and the Setting

After 1880, immigration to the United States increased rapidly in response to the enticing offers of manfacturers, as well as the allure of America to people of other countries as a land of security if not a land of plenty. A national study of new problems arising from immigration, conducted in 1907 by the International Committee of the YMCA, showed a drastic shift in countries of origin of immigrants: before 1880, largely from the British Isles, Scandinavia, and north central Europe; after 1880, largely from Italy, eastern Europe, and Asia. The same study showed that seventy percent of the immigrants stayed in New England, New York, New Jersey, and Pennsylvania. An earlier survey demonstrated that most of these new citizens stayed in cities; in 1890, for example, there were 657,000 "foreign born" in Massachusetts, and 601,000 of them were urban dwellers.

To the city of Boston, port of entry second only to New York, the wave of immigration from the 1840's to the end of the century was decisive. In fifty years the balance of population shifted conspicuously.

M. A. DeWolfe Howe recorded in 1903 a striking contrast between 1845 and 1899 in four groups of the constituency of the population of Boston. In 1845, those living in Boston but born in other parts of the United States ranked first in number; second were those born in Boston of American parentage; third, those of foreign birth and origin; and fourth, the children of foreign born parents. In 1899 the pattern was reversed: foreign born people constituted the largest element in the population of Boston; children of foreign born parents were second in number; those born in other parts of the United States were third; and those born in Boston of American parentage were fourth.

Here is the basis of the comments by Boston writers of the 1890's—comments sometimes humorous, sometimes bitter—that the "Yankee" was doomed to extinction. Certainly the population of Boston was changing, as a part of the changing American scene.

5

At the same time, new directions were showing in the activity and movement of the "native" population. From the discovery of gold in California at mid-century until the 1870's there had been a conspicuous migration from New England westward; in 1853, for example, 149 ships filled with prospectors for gold left the port of Boston. Large numbers of farm boys and family men followed the advice traditionally credited to Horace Greeley to "go west," not only to find gold but to explore the frontier and establish new homes, as bold New Englanders had been doing since the period of colonial expansion.

Then the gold fever abated, and in 1890 a pronouncement from Washington stated that there was no more free government land—there was no longer an American "frontier."

Restless, ambitious boys on New England farms thereafter found an outlet for their energy and dissatisfaction by going to the city, and for those in the northern states, Boston was the obvious city. In Boston, they believed, they would find good jobs at high pay, and they would enjoy diversions which a small town could not offer.

The Gay Nineties have perhaps been given a glamor they do not deserve yet the appeal of electric lights, gaming rooms, and saloons must have been strong to country boys of the time. Burlesque added to the gaiety of the '90's and in Boston was a popular entertainment, with the Black Crook Burlesquers, the Bon-Ton Burlesquers, and other companies advertised in the daily press as "beautiful, dazzling, bewitching." Baseball games, bicycle races, excursions to Nantasket, and encounters between great-name fighters like Corbett and McCoy varied the local activity and the news from other cities. Revere Beach attracted crowds estimated as high as 100,000 on summer Sundays. In some respects the decade was limited, but for energetic young men it provided excitement and pleasure—good, bad, and indifferent.

The younger generation in Boston from 1890 to 1900 was made up of diverse groups and elements, resulting from changing times and shifting population.

The Time and the Setting

There was still a strong vestige of the Yankee population, secure families with sons carefully brought up, and educated, at Harvard or one of the other colleges in the area, for the law or another profession in keeping with the family tradition and heritage.

More conspicuous, both in numbers and in driving energy, were the young men recently arrived from other countries, or the sons of immigrants. Some of them were fortunate enough to go to college; most of them were forced by economic necessity to begin working at an early age in men's jobs.

Reinforcing the second group were the young men from outlying towns and the states of northern New England. Many of them settled down to hard work and dull leisure, if they resisted the blandishments of bright lights and easy pleasures. Those who had ambition and stamina were ready and willing to improve themselves by occupying their spare time profitably, by accumulating knowledge and skill that would help them to advance in business, trade, or profession.

In theory, advanced education was readily available, for Boston had become a center of education. The period 1850 to 1890, and especially the decade following the Civil War, was a time of birth for many schools and colleges. Twelve present day institutions of higher learning in the Greater Boston area—including three theological seminaries, the New England Conservatory of Music, the Massachusetts School of Art, and such familiar colleges as Radcliffe, Boston University, Boston College, Massachusetts Institute of Technology, and Wellesley College—were founded in this period. In Massachusetts beyond the Boston area, seven collegiate institutions were established during the same forty years. This new generation of schools and colleges, added to older institutions like Harvard, Tufts, Williams, Amherst, and Mt. Holyoke, provided higher education for the increasing number of young people who were completing secondary school and were interested in going beyond that point.

Yet in practice, college was available only to the fortunate

7

few who by virtue of family tradition and financial support could afford the luxury of four years of leisurely education and attendant heavy costs.

Moreover, the old colleges of Massachusetts and those established during the last half of the nineteenth century were conventional institutions, built in the pattern and following the tradition of New England education, and back of that the kind of education that had gone on for centuries in the mother country. Colleges were intended to prepare young men for the professions and for related scholarly pursuits; they also prepared a few young women for teaching.

The readiness of Boston in the 1890's for an outward spread and diversification of educational opportunities is demonstrated by the founding of Simmons College.

In 1870 John Simmons wrote above his signature, "It is my will to found and endow an institution to be called Simmons Female College, for the purpose of teaching medicine, music, drawing, designing, telegraphy, and other branches of art, science, and industry best calculated to enable the scholars to acquire an independent livelihood."

The actual founding of Simmons College was delayed for thirty years by the Great Fire of 1872, which wiped out the buildings in downtown Boston from which a fund of a half million dollars was to accumulate. Simmons College of 1899, started under much more restricted terms than Mr. Simmons' original broad intentions but still designed to prepare young women for independent livelihood, was more appropriate to the 1890's than to the 1870's. For capable, ambitious, and respectable young women, training in vocational skills was made possible by the founding of Simmons College.

For the same category of young men the Boston Young Men's Christian Association was providing at that time lectures and classes that would lead ultimately to the development of a university.

II

AN EVENING INSTITUTE FOR
YOUNG MEN

In May of 1896 the Directors of the Boston Young Men's Christian Association voted to establish an "Evening Institute for Young Men" and to employ a director to organize and develop it. The purpose of the new institute was to merge, coordinate, and improve the effectiveness of the classes which had evolved over a period of forty years of unorganized but consistent efforts at providing part-time and supplementary education for young men. To the history of Northeastern University this decision by the Directors is an important antecedent event.

At its formation in 1851, the Boston YMCA, the first in the United States and following by a month the organization of a YMCA in Montreal, included in its articles of incorporation and by-laws authorization of "a committee on lectures, whose duty it is to procure teachers and lecturers for any private classes that may be formed by the members."

For some years there were more lecturers than teachers, although an early Literary Class, later called the Lyceum, had a varied but continuous activity for more than two decades. In 1875, Dr. George E. Hatton gave $5000 "to provide instruction for young men," and thus became the first financial sponsor of the educational work of the YMCA. Perhaps because of that specific contribution, in the following year the Committee on Lectures became the Committee on Instruction. By 1882 the

Boylston Street Building of the Boston YMCA — first home of Northeastern — built in 1883, destroyed by fire in 1910

Committee was offering ten courses of twenty lessons each, and the YMCA Annual Report records the fact that 765 course tickets were taken by members and an additional 144 by ladies.

In 1896 the time and conditions were ripe for a systematic development of the educational efforts that had built up through the years. The Association was well settled in its building at the corner of Berkeley and Boylston Streets, completed in 1883 and described in the following year as "unique in architecture, simple in design, warm in color, and beautiful in its proportions." It was the fourth headquarters of the Boston YMCA and the second building which it had owned.

10

An Evening Institute for Young Men

The Association was justifiably proud of the facilities and activities provided for its members. It publicized the advantages of the library, socials, song sessions, Bible classes, private shower and sponge baths, a bicycle storage room with free checking, hand ball, exercise rooms, and a running track of twenty-eight laps to the mile. A gymnasium program under the direction of Robert Jeffries Roberts gave opportunity for physical development, with a doctor in attendance to examine new members and make recommendations as to form and extent of exercise. The winter of 1896–1897 offered "Sixteen Superior Entertainments," free to members, with such diverse programs as illustrated lectures on India and Mexico; dramatic and humorous readings; the Brown University Glee, Banjo, and Mandolin Clubs; the Salem Cadet Band; and Tyrolean and Swiss Warblers in native costume.

Against this background of activity and opportunity, the 1896–1897 Annual Prospectus of the Boston YMCA announced the new Young Men's Evening Institute, with the promise "A good education possible to every young man." An Association membership entitled "any young man of moral character" to Institute courses and all other privileges of the YMCA except the use of the gymnasium, although the membership did include the use of bathing facilities.

Frank Palmer Speare was engaged to become Educational Director of the Boston YMCA and to be in charge of the Evening Institute. At the age of twenty-seven, Mr. Speare was committed to education, in spite of the fact that the family tradition was sea-going, his father a steamship builder and operator, and a pioneer in the development of electric telegraphy, as well as weather bureau and transportation service in the United States and South America.

In 1896 Mr. Speare had completed his education in the public schools of Boston, Chauncey Hall School, and Bridgewater Normal School, and was taking courses at Harvard College, where he sought advice as to the wisdom of assuming the position which the YMCA had offered him. He also had had

11

practical experience in education, as principal of Avon High School, a teacher in Berkeley School (which carried on its work in the YMCA building), director of an evening school program in the city of Medford, and teacher of English for one year in the Boston YMCA courses.

The records indicate that Mr. Speare undertook the direction of the Evening Institute with the high-minded optimism, enthusiasm, and imagination which marked his long service to the YMCA and to Northeastern University. Thirty courses were offered in the first year, including algebra, bookkeeping, drawing, electricity, French, German, Latin, geography, literature, music, penmanship, physiology, and stenography. Seventeen instructors were listed in the Institute announcement, and Mr. Speare himself taught classes in algebra, arithmetic, and English. In addition, the Institute promoted a banjo club, camera club, orchestra, and a Young Men's Congress devoted to weekly parliamentary debates and discussions.

The first year of the new venture was successful. The Directors of the YMCA reported with satisfaction that Mr. Speare had instituted important changes, with the approval of the Board. The International YMCA Committee's outline of study was adopted, classes were reduced in size, regular examinations were required, reports on attendance and class progress were required from teachers, some classes were increased from one session to two sessions a week, lockers were provided for books and drawing tools, and tuition was increased from two dollars to five dollars. This increase reduced the total number of students but resulted in more regularity of attendance and a larger number completing their series of classes. An earlier financial arrangement had been a deposit of one dollar, returned to the student if he attended seventy-five percent of the class sessions. Even with this pleasant provision the number of young men completing courses had at times been disappointingly small.

At the end of the second year the YMCA Board considered among the needs of the future a scholarship fund for "worthy persons who are unable to pay even the moderate charges required in our Evening Institute," and suggested that $15,000 as invested funds would yield enough income to meet the need. A department of music had been added to provide study in theory and composition as well as voice and instrumentation. Courses had been set up to prepare young men for civil service examinations and for higher education. More important in view of later developments was a series of law classes sponsored by the Lowell Institute but conducted by the Evening Institute.

In two years the Evening Institute for Young Men fulfilled its assignment of organizing and co-ordinating a group of diffuse and unrelated courses, and at the same time worked toward the establishment of educational programs that would be preparatory and terminal rather than incidental and supplementary.

III

THE FOUNDING OF SCHOOLS

The School of Law, 1898

"Special courses by the Lowell Institute under the auspices of the YMCA" were announced for the fall of 1897. The special courses were Elementary Electricity, Advanced Electricity, and Law, the last to meet for two-hour sessions on two evenings a week with instructors, three in number, from the Boston University Law School. The announcement said further, "it is hoped that the attendance and interest shown will justify the addition of advanced courses the following year."

The attendance and interest seem to have demonstrated a real need for additional opportunity for legal study in Boston. Two law schools were available. Harvard, in 1817, had been the first university in the country to undertake an academic law program. Boston University established its law school in 1872. By the mid-90's the combined enrollment of students of law at the two institutions totaled about 750. The fact that these two schools could not adequately meet the need of the time is indicated by two cumulative changes.

The time-honored method of preparing for the bar by reading law in the office of an established lawyer or law firm had begun to lose its effectiveness. Legal knowledge had become increasingly extensive and at the same time specialized, with the result that at the end of his apprenticeship the legal as-

14

pirant might well be limited in his total knowledge of the law, and restricted in competence to the one phase of law on which the guiding lawyer or office concentrated.

The industrial and commercial growth of Boston was resulting in increased opportunities for young men with general legal knowledge, as well as for practicing lawyers. Court officials and clerks with facility in legal fact and terminology were needed. At many points the demand was not being met by the supply.

Mr. Speare showed skill and enterprise in launching a full-fledged program of legal study as one of his many undertakings. He secured the support of the Hon. James R. Dunbar, a distinguished judge; Samuel C. Bennett, Dean of the Boston University Law School; and James Barr Ames, Dean of the Harvard Law School. These men agreed to act as an Advisory Committee, to plan the course of study, to pass judgment on instructors, and to supervise the operation of the new evening law school. Mr. Speare also found students who committed themselves to taking the advanced courses and paying the increased tuition.

After these and other preparatory steps, all approved with some reluctance by the Board of Directors of the YMCA, the "Department of Law of the Boston YMCA" was announced. It offered two hundred hours of instruction, in one-hour sessions, four evenings a week. The first faculty consisted of five men—three with Harvard training and two from Boston University—teaching courses in Pleading, Property, Criminal Law, Contracts, and Torts. The tuition was announced as $30 a year, including a five dollar YMCA membership.

The new program started on October 3, 1898, a significant date in the story of Northeastern. For Boston and the world it was a day of vigorous and varied activity.

The Boston *Globe* of Sunday, October 2, and Monday, October 3, records major and minor events, and reflects the spirit of the time.

In Paris, American and Spanish commissioners were in session to arrange final terms following the brief Spanish-American War. Paris, at the same time, was reported to be "in turmoil all day" over the Dreyfus Case. On the other side of the globe, "threatening conditions" in China had led to an order from Washington to Admiral Dewey, to send two warships from Manila to a position as close as possible to Pekin. At Vancouver a ship arrived carrying gold nuggets from the Klondike valued at a half million dollars.

News of special immediate interest to Boston was the grounding on foggy Sandy Hook of the three-masted schooner *Stephen Bennett*, the preparations of the Ancient and Honorable Artillery Company for their ceremonious expedition to Quebec, and the Saturday football scores, with Harvard defeating Williams, 11 to 0, and Yale triumphant over Wesleyan, 5 to 0.

Crime was even then a problem, for a bicyclist in West Roxbury was relieved of the single dollar he had at the time, and a man captured by the police in the Back Bay was found to have a cache of razors, jewelry, and money in his room indicating that perhaps he had committed a series of thefts and holdups.

In some respects the year 1898 was a year simple and remote from our time, as evidenced by the advertisement of "best creamery butter" at $1.05 for a five-pound box, and the sports department of Jordan Marsh & Co. offering golf balls at $2 a dozen and clubs at $1 each. Yet the repetition of history is suggested by the Uncle Dudley editorial in the Sunday *Globe*, on Colonel Theodore Roosevelt as a unique figure in American history, moving from the military to the political scene.

Recreation and diversion in Boston were varied in the early days of October, 1898. At the more refined and restrained theaters the offerings were impressive. Maude Adams was acting in *The Little Minister* at the Hollis St. Theatre, and Anna Held in *The French Maid* at the Park Theatre. *The Great Diamond Robbery* was at the Castle Square Theatre, *Way Down East* at the Tremont Theatre, and at the Boston Theatre a repertory company, the Bostonians, was presenting *Robin Hood.* Other attractions were a horse show, and a War Exposition at Boston Auditorium on Tremont Street. Brockton Fair offered displays and exhibits, vaudeville, horse races, and a midway, all for an admission price of fifty cents.

Against this background and in the face of this competition, law courses were started at the YMCA.

The first lecture in the new program was delivered on the evening of Monday, October 3, by Robert Gray Dodge, teacher of the course in Property. Mr. Dodge was then a young man of twenty-six. He had completed his undergraduate work at Harvard and had received his law degree in 1897. In the spring of the following year he had taken over the teaching of a course at the Harvard Law School, when a member of the faculty became ill; he was engaged to continue teaching on a regular basis in 1898–1899.

Nevertheless, teaching in a new, untried evening school of law was another matter. Sixty years later, Mr. Dodge remembered the occasion of October 3, 1898, as a terrifying one, faced as he was by a class of thirty of his contemporaries and elders, and with Dean Bennett and Dean Ames of the Advisory Committee sitting on either side of the teacher to observe and evaluate.

Yet the first lecture and those that followed were successful. The law program was under way, as a planned, supervised course of study directed toward two related, predetermined objectives: preparation for the bar examination of the Commonwealth of Massachusetts, and an accumulation of legal knowledge for professional use in business, court procedure, and other areas of work. This pattern marked a new phase in the educational program of the Boston YMCA and the founding of Northeastern University.

The growth and development of the program of legal study during the next six years is reflected by the data submitted to the Committee on Education of the Massachusetts Legislature when in 1904 the Evening Law School asked for the right to incorporate the school and to grant a degree in law.

The statement reported that 662 men had been enrolled since October of 1898; forty-two men had been graduated in the two classes of 1902 and 1903, and thirty-seven of those graduates had been admitted to the bar.

The educational background of the 235 students then in the Law School reflects a surprising range and diversity. Twenty were college graduates, from Harvard College, Boston University, Amherst College, Brown University, University of Nebraska, Cambridge University, M.I.T., Stevens Institute, and Tufts Dental College. Nineteen had attended colleges spread geographically from Boston College to Prince of Wales College in Canada. In contrast, eighty-four students of law "had attended high school," twenty-three were grammar school graduates, and the name of one student carried the notation "never attended school, but possessed of extraordinary ability."

An occupational tabulation lists students from thirty-five trades and vocations, with a preponderance of law clerks, clerks in comercial houses, bookkeepers, merchants, and salesmen.

Through action of the General Court of the Commonwealth the "Evening Law School of the Boston Young Men's Christian Association" was incorporated in 1904, with power to grant the LL.B. degree. Twenty degrees were awarded in 1904 and 1905. Mr. Speare acted as the first Dean of the Law School, and carried the title until 1920, when he was succeeded by Everett A. Churchill.

Throughout its history, the Law School made a valuable contribution to the educational life of Boston. It became a large school; Albert Bushnell Hart's history of Massachusetts cites the enrollment of 1926–1927 as 2440. Changes were made along the way to meet changing needs. Divisions were established in Worcester and Springfield in 1919 and in Providence in 1920. In the following year Austin W. Scott of the Harvard Law School made a study and report which recommended that women should not be disqualified for admission, saying, "There seems to be no good reason why women should not be admitted to the Law School. In all of the leading law schools, except Harvard and Columbia, women are now admitted." In September of 1922 women students were accepted in the Boston school and in Worcester and Springfield. A final change of location took place in 1938 when the Law School was moved from Huntington Avenue to Beacon Hill; at the same time, day classes, with an initial enrollment of seventeen, were started.

In the evolution of Northeastern University, the Law School represents the early and successful exploration of possibilities of study, in the evening and under adverse conditions, leading to a degree and to recognize educational status.

The Automobile School, 1903

At the turn of the century the automobile was in its infant stage but few infants in American history have matured, or at least grown, so fast or with such far-reaching effects.

The exact time of the origin of the automobile is still a matter of disagreement; it seems fairly certain, however, that on this side of the Atlantic the first successful production of self-propelled road vehicles took place in 1893 and immediately thereafter. The new miracle was soon named, by the French Academy, after other groups and many individuals had suggested such labels as "quadricycle," "automotor," "petrocar," and "autocycle."

Within ten years an industry was in progress and the American way of life was beginning to change. Production and use of the automobile expanded at an astonishing rate. M. M. Musselman in his history of the automobile in America records the production of cars in 1896 as totaling eight, with sixteen cars registered in the country, though he points out that a few unlicensed automobiles probably were operating. In 1900, production had risen to 4,192, and registration to 8,000; in 1910, production was 181,000 and registration 468,500.

Massachusetts was the scene of significant activity in this early period of the automobile. The Duryea brothers of Springfield produced a functioning horseless carriage in 1893, the same year in which Elwood Haynes of Indiana brought out his. In 1897 the Stanley brothers rode through the streets of Newton, to the astonishment of neighbors and horses, in a lightweight buggy propelled by a steam engine weighing 750 pounds. The first automobile show in New England was held at Mechanics Hall in the following year; it consisted of four cars—a sports car from France, and three American cars, one gasolene, one steam, one electric.

The early 1900's were expanding years in the history of the automobile. In 1902 the American Automobile Association was organized and soon issued the famous "Blue Books," which, in the years before numbered highway routes, directed motorists from coast to coast by citing distances and making directional references to white churches, red barns, watering troughs, and sawmills. In 1903, Henry Ford and eleven venturesome investors formed the Ford Motor Co., and began producing a vehicle known for a time as Fordmobile.

Also in 1903, the Boston YMCA opened "The Automobile School of the Evening Institute." The announcement promised three courses: A. (open to ladies and gentlemen) a "series of lectures for owners, prospective purchasers, chauffeurs, machinists, and others interested in motor traction"; B. (for men only) a "drafting course for draftsmen and machinists who wish to enter the automobile industry"; C. (for men only) a "shop course in the mechanism, adjustment, handling, and care of steam, gasolene, and electric Automobile motors." A teaching staff of five men was to be supplemented by an Advisory Board of six, including the president of the Massachusetts Auto Club.

The first year of the school, though a school of theory because of lack of space and equipment, appears to have been successful. The Directors of the YMCA in their report recorded the fact that the new courses "attracted a number of prospective buyers, so that the class contained men of great wealth and social position, as well as those from the humbler walks of life." The first classes were attended by "more than 250," and an undocumented but persistent tradition suggests that the early lecturers wore formal evening dress in the classroom. In later years, by way of contrast, there is some indication that both class members and teachers in the school were regarded as roughnecks by those in other schools.

Within a year, branches of the Automobile School were established in Worcester, Providence, Springfield, and Brockton, with instructors sent out from Boston. Similar schools were started by other organizations in New York, Detroit, Buffalo, and San Francisco, but the Automobile School of the Evening Institute carried the designation "the first school of its kind in the world."

The prospectus of 1905 announced the purchase of a "fine 10 h.p. White steam touring car" and a "16 h.p. Peerless touring car." Mounted wheels, tires, and repair kits were available, and a course of driving lessons was offered, to qualify the motorist for securing his license from the Highway Commission. Shop work was made possible by the use of rented space in the Park Square Auto Station. Later, the work was conducted in the White Garage on Newbury Street, in a building on Harcourt Street, and finally, in 1911, in the new Vocational Building on St. Botolph Street, erected by the YMCA before the construction of its main building on Huntington Avenue.

The Automobile School was clearly a vocational rather than an academic enterprise. It performed a real service in the early years of motor transportation, when the horseless carriage was a strange and mysterious vehicle. It interested "men of great wealth," instructed mechanics, and insured the future of coachmen to Boston families by converting them to the status of chauffeur. As the years passed, the name of the school was changed to "Automotive School," to "Automobile Engineering School," and back to "Automobile School." The leadership of the school changed often; Galen D. Light, who filled so many positions during the early years of the development of Northeastern, is listed as Superintendent of the Automobile School in 1907.

For twenty-three years the Automobile School served its purpose. It was discontinued in 1926, when the Vocational Building was remodeled to become the Laboratory Building, to provide space for the work of the School of Engineering.

The Evening Polytechnic School, 1904

In an effort to systematize further the work of the Evening Institute, Mr. Speare, and Mr. Light, Assistant Educational Director, undertook the establishment of departments and schools. In addition to the Law School, three groupings of courses resulted in what was referred to as a "university basis of organization."

The General School offered courses in Language, Grammar, Music, Commercial subjects, English, and Oratory. The Preparatory School gave courses directed toward college entrance and Civil Service examinations.

The Evening Polytechnic School was a reorganization of technical courses old and new. The array of offerings was extensive—Art, Architecture, Automobile Engineering, Chemistry, Clay Modeling, Designing, Higher Mathematics, Marine Engineering, Naval Architecture, Navigation, Seamanship, Steam and Structural Engineering, and Surveying.

Further specialization took place in the following year, 1905, when the Automobile School was withdrawn from the Polytechnic School to become a separate unit again, and a School of Advertising and a School of Applied Electricity and Steam Engineering were started.

Year by year, courses and curricula were moved from one school to another as the technical work of the Institute expanded to meet the growing need for men trained in mechanics, electricity, surveying, and related skills. By 1907 the

Polytechnic School, under the direction of Dean Franklin T. Kurt, encompassed theoretical study and shop work adequate to the requirements of the time.

The Evening Polytechnic School was a part of the educational structure for over twenty years. In 1921 it offered three years of study leading to diplomas in Civil, Mechanical, Electrical, Chemical, Structural, Industrial, and Automotive Engineering; and the work was conducted by branches in Worcester, Springfield, New Haven, and Bridgeport, as well as in Boston.

Lincoln Institute was formed in 1927 to carry on the technical courses of the Polytechnic School. In the meantime, a parallel development from the Polytechnic School had become the first day college of Northeastern University.

The School of Commerce and Finance, 1907

Vocational training for commerce and industry was among the first educational undertakings of the Boston YMCA. Courses in typewriting, shorthand, penmanship, and bookkeeping appear in the early records.

As the ambitious developments of the Evening Institute were planned and launched, Mr. Speare, supported by his associates in a belief that young men should be helped to prepare themselves for whatever work they were capable of doing, decided that training could be provided for more responsible positions in business than those of clerk or secretary.

Academic training for business was still a new phenomenon in American education. The University of Pennsylvania had established its Wharton School of Commerce and Finance in 1881. The Amos Tuck School of Administration and Finance at Dartmouth College began its work in 1900, the same year of the founding of the New York University School of Commerce, Accounts, and Finance; and the latter was primarily an evening school for employed people. In 1908, business courses were initiated at Harvard University as a department of the Graduate School of Arts and Sciences, and thereby gave rise to the Harvard Business School.

These developments moved forward against the resistance of skepticism and open criticism. Conservative educational thinkers, especially in New England with its long tradition of classical education, viewed with disapproval the intrusion of courses directed toward success in business. They suggested that the purpose of such courses was merely to enable young men to make more money for themselves, and implied that the means by which those young men would make money might well prove to be devious and dubious.

As late as 1935, Alfred North Whitehead, in his conversations with Lucien Price, said, ". . . law has been civilized—that was done by the Greeks and Romans, Justinian and that lot;— medicine has been taken out of magic; education has been getting rid of its humbug; and next it is time to teach business its sociological function; for if America is to be civilized, it must be done (at least for the present) by the business class, who are in possession of the power and the economic processes. I don't need to tell you that there is a good deal of sniffing on this, the Harvard College and graduate schools side of the Charles River, sniffing at the new Harvard School of Business Administration on the opposite bank. That strikes me as snobbish and unimaginative. If the American universities were up to their job they would be taking business in hand and teaching it ethics and professional standards."

Nevertheless, as American business progressed from the period of tycoons and robber barons to a period of corporations, small enterprises, and sole proprietorships, the value of academic training for business slowly came to be accepted. The Evening Institute was in the vanguard of a movement toward establishing business as a profession, with techniques and skills, concepts and standards which would come to mark business as a growing science rather than a trade.

The School of Commerce and Finance was initiated in 1907

with departments of Commerce, Finance, Administration, Business Law, and Languages. These departments undertook to give systematic programs of study in Commerce, Finance, and Accounting. Like the other schools, this addition to the "university" structure of the Institute was modified from time to time; later fields of specialization, for example, were banking, business administration, finance and bond salesmanship, and accounting. From the start, however, the school required four years of evening study for the completion of a program in any of the specialized areas.

At the end of its first three years of operation, in 1910, the School of Commerce and Finance was incorporated, and in the following year was authorized by the General Court to grant the degrees of Bachelor and Master of Commercial Science.

In 1928 the school became the School of Business, with Carl D. Smith as its Dean. Thereafter it developed into the largest school of the Evening Division of Northeastern University, with subsequent changes in degree-granting privileges, and the addition of graduate work in 1950.

The Association Day School, 1909

Space, in the literal, physical sense, was one of the major problems of the growing Association Institute. In the early years, a class was formed whenever there were young men interested in attending the class; then a room was found in which the class could meet. Later, when the program had outgrown the available areas in the YMCA building on Berkeley Street— and even more drastically when that building burned—classrooms were borrowed from M.I.T., the School Department of the City of Boston, and the Boston Young Men's Christian Union. Classrooms and other working areas were rented for temporary use. Still later, space became a matter of land, on which to build and establish a permanent home for a new university.

A contrasting effect of physical space on the development of the Institute occurred when Chauncey Hall School, which had carried on its work in the YMCA building, moved to other quarters. Mr. Speare, always interested in new developments, proposed to the YMCA authorities that empty rooms could be used to educational and financial advantage for daytime classes conducted by the Institute.

A broader motivation in the establishment of the Association Day School was the recognition of the need for a new kind of college preparatory school. The announcement of the Association Day School as available to boys "who, for various reasons, do not find public and high-priced private schools suited to their needs or means" was the result of careful analysis and planning. The intention was to provide a college preparatory program under conditions which would make possible the supervision and direction of students as individuals, a fusion of the influences of home and school in forming and developing character, and a program of sports and other activities which would direct toward maturity the growth of intelligent and promising boys.

In specific and practical terms, the school, as a non-profit organization within a department of the YMCA, intended to provide college preparation at costs midway between those of the private boarding and day schools then available in the Boston area, and schools giving evening preparatory work to supplement and reinforce high school education.

The Evening Institute had from its beginning conducted college preparatory work. Young men were qualified for college by certificate, and prepared to take entrance examinations. As early as 1897, eighteen students passed from the Institute to colleges of good standing.

In 1909 the college preparatory work was reorganized and established as a program of daytime study. With an opening enrollment of one hundred, the school soon expanded to a student body of 250, and has maintained that level down to the present time, in keeping with the original commitment of conducting a school in which personal relations between teacher and student are a major objective.

When, in 1913, the educational work of the YMCA was settled in the new building on Huntington Avenue, the "Association Day School" became "The Huntington School for Boys." As a day school for commuting students it came to be recognized as a college preparatory school of high academic standards, competent administration, and successful results in directing and developing individual students. It built up a substantial program of general activities and of sports; Huntington teams in basketball, track, and swimming have competed for many years with other preparatory school teams and college freshman teams.

After the incorporation of Northeastern College in 1916, the Huntington School was one of the Northeastern group of schools. By 1950 it had become apparent that Northeastern could best devote its efforts to education at the college level. Consequently, The Huntington School became a Branch of the Boston YMCA, and continued to do the work assigned to the "Association Day School" forty-one years earlier.

The Co-operative Engineering School, 1909

Each of the undertakings of the Evening Institute required initiative, imagination, and optimism. Some of the experiments were short-lived, as evidenced by the "schools" which came and went during the early 1900's; others became major contributions to educational progress in New England.

Co-operative education in an academic setting was established at the University of Cincinnati in 1906, through the pioneer efforts of Dean Herman Schneider. Essentially the plan was a modernization of the ancient apprentice system, adapted to the needs of industry and the training of technical workers in the twentieth century. After a single-handed campaign to overcome the reluctance of industry and the conservatism of academic thinking, Mr. Schneider started twenty-seven students on six-year curricula in mechanical, electrical, and chemical engineering, alternating week by week between classroom and work in Cincinnati companies.

It is impossible to know why the Boston YMCA initiated the second program of co-operative education in the United States. The "Cincinnati Plan" was receiving attention and comment, both favorable and unfavorable, and it is probable that Mr. Speare saw the plan as an interesting challenge and another opportunity for development. Clearly the plan would provide technical training for young men who because of limited financial status were unable to pay the costs of education at the established schools of engineering, and these were the young men in whom the Institute had been interested since its founding. The appeal of "earn while you learn" was a strong one.

For the fall of 1909 the Polytechnic School, then directed by Dean Hercules W. Geromanos, announced "Co-Operative Engineering Courses." A four-year daytime program would consist of alternating single weeks of classroom study and practical work on jobs. Companies which had already agreed in advance to accept students as workers, with two students maintaining one work assignment, were the Boston and Maine Railroad, Boston and Albany Railroad, Boston Consolidated Gas Company, and Boston Elevated Railway Company.

Eight students enrolled in the first year of the experiment, and the Co-operative Plan was underway in Boston.

In 1910, curricula in Civil and Mechanical Engineering and in Chemistry were announced. The student enrollment advanced to thirty, and eight companies employed students on co-operative work jobs. In that year, Carl S. Ell, a graduate student at M.I.T., became a part-time teacher of surveying.

The catalog of 1912–1913 used the name "Co-Operative Engineering School," with curricula in Civil, Mechanical, Electrical, and Chemical Engineering. The faculty had developed to a roster of eighteen, the student body to seventy, and the co-operating companies to ten. School expenses, including YMCA membership, were announced as $100 for the year, rooms in the dormitory of the new YMCA building were available at $1.50 and up, and board in 1912 was costing $3.50 to $5.00 a week. Co-operative students were earning from five to six dollars a week during a thirty-week working year, on a pay scale "by agreement with co-operative firms" of ten cents per hour in the first year, and by systematic gradations up to sixteen cents per hour in the fourth year. In addition to their technical subjects, all students in the engineering majors were required to take two years of Business English, and the Chemical majors studied, also, two years of German.

In 1917, Mr. Ell, who had been Assistant Dean of Engineering since 1914, succeeded Mr. Geromanos as Dean of the "Co-operative School of Engineering." The catalog of the following year lists forty-two co-operating companies and a student body of 235. Evidences of growing college life are a yearbook, the *Cauldon*; a monthly student newspaper, the *Co-op*, started in 1916; and professional societies for students in the four branches of engineering.

World War I was necessarily a disrupting interlude in the progress of the school. In 1920, however, the engineering student body was 592, with ninety-two companies providing jobs for them. Tuition had advanced to $175, plus an activities fee of ten dollars. Activities now included the additions of a Glee Club, Orchestra, and teams in baseball and basketball; the *Co-op* was issued twice a month.

By action of the General Court in March of 1920, Northeastern College, of which the Co-operative Engineering School was the most substantial part, was empowered to grant engineering curricula degrees—B.C.E., B.M.E., B.E.E., B.Ch.E. A fifth curriculum, "Administrative Engineering," was added in the following year, and changed to "Industrial Engineering" in 1928.

Later modifications in curricula and plan, including the adoption of ten-week alternating periods of work and study and the extension of the program from four to five years, resulted in the enhanced status of the school, reflected by changes in the degrees granted, accreditation of the professional curricula, and a wider acceptance of the co-operative plan of education.

Northeastern's "College of Engineering," so named in 1936, is another result of experiment which by virtue of careful planning and persistent development proved to be of enduring value.

IV

FORMING AN EDUCATIONAL
PATTERN

The first two decades of the present century represent, in the history of Northeastern, a period of adaptation, development, and progress. Development and progress were difficult. Extensions of courses and curricula were made in a setting of limited space, facilities, and finances. Advances in educational stability and status were made under the same handicaps, further complicated by a reluctance on the part of some elements in educational Boston to accept a YMCA Evening Institute as a developing college.

Support came from many directions—the men who assisted the Law School in its early years; M.I.T. President Richard MacLaurin and Dean Gardner C. Anthony of Tufts College, who were interested in and helpful to the development of the Co-operative School of Engineering; other educators and public figures, including Andrey A. Potter, Dean of the Schools of Engineering, Purdue University, from 1920 to 1953; and institutions and organizations which provided housing for YMCA and Northeastern classes, sometimes for financial consideration but often as a gesture of good will and encouragement.

The disapproval and resistance came from other men and other institutions, especially when the new Northeastern College petitioned the General Court for the right to grant degrees. The concept of YMCA classes for working people was an admirable one; the recognition and acceptance of an ambitious but ill equipped and unendowed college was another matter.

During this period of about twenty years, the destiny of Northeastern was determined by the combined efforts of a group of exceptional men.

American colleges and universities have been founded and fostered in many different ways, ranging from the dedicated pioneer work of sectarian zealots to the munificent financial gesture of a single man. One of the unusual ingredients in the evolution of Northeastern University is the assembling, by chance and by selection, of a combination of men with diverse talents and varying motivations who worked together, sometimes against their individual inclinations, to make possible the creation of a university.

The men who helped to formulate Northeastern are numerous. Some of them were unaware of the direction the results of their work would ultimately take; others worked consistently toward a predetermined end.

Arthur S. Johnson, President of the Boston Young Men's Christian Association from 1897 to 1929, and George W. Mehaffey, General Secretary from 1895 to 1919, were guiding and controlling forces in the early years of the Evening Institute and the founding of Northeastern.

Hercules W. Geromanos, a graduate of M.I.T. in 1902 who came to the Evening Polytechnic School in 1909, was important to the launching of the Co-operative Plan for daytime engineering study and its development until 1917.

William Lincoln Smith began teaching in the Educational Department of the YMCA in 1895, was Dean of the School of Practical Electricity in 1908, and after holding other positions became Head of the Department of Electrical Engineering in the Co-operative School of Engineering in 1912. Professor Smith was a teacher of science who illuminated science with classical learning and nineteenth-century gentlemanly decorum. He was awarded the honorary degree of Eng.D. by Northeastern in 1937, at the time he retired from the Chairmanship of the Department of Electrical Engineering. He continued to teach until the year before his death in 1947.

These are four representative men of the formative period which extends from evening classes to an established university.

In that period, four other men are of paramount significance in their effect on the evolution of Northeastern. As with the total group, these four contributed varying gifts, interests, and objectives; working together they constituted a complementary group which in the larger sense made possible the development of a university. The men are, in order of their association with the educational work, Frank Palmer Speare, Galen David Light, Carl Stephens Ell, and Everett Avery Churchill.

Frank Palmer Speare

In 1940, Dr. Speare retired as President of Northeastern University, to become President Emeritus. That date ended a period of forty-four years with the Boston YMCA and Northeastern, but did not mark either the beginning or the termination of his activity in education. He had been a teacher and administrator for several years before he joined the YMCA as Educational Director in 1896, and he continued as Chairman of the Board, President, and Director of Chandler School until 1947.

When Dr. Speare died in May of 1954, at the age of eighty-five, the statement of his successor at Northeastern, President Ell, summarized not only facts but the feeling of many people throughout New England:

"Dr. Frank Palmer Speare was, without question, an outstanding leader. It was his indomitable enthusiasm and optimism which made Northeastern possible in the early days in the face of many discouraging experiences which met the development of the educational work which is now Northeastern University.

"He was the guiding spirit in the establishment of the School of Law, the first school in the University system; and it was his inspiring personal traits which led others in directing, molding, and executing in a practical way the ideas and suggestions which he conceived from time to time.

"A man with a bright, alert mind brimful of ideas and sparkling with enthusiasm, the first President of Northeastern University will forever have a unique and honored place in the history of the great educational institution which his leadership guided through its early days.

"Dr. Speare had a keen sense of humor and thoroughly enjoyed people. He referred frequently to 'the great satisfaction of feeling that I have made some contribution to American youth.' He fondly recalled the start of the University by remarking: 'We started with an eraser and two sticks of chalk'— a fact which is literally true.

"When asked about the factors in the success of the University, Dr. Speare pointed out repeatedly: 'The reason for the success of Northeastern was teamwork. The perseverance of the Trustees, who gave liberally of their time and money; skilled administrative officers; loyal and devoted faculty and assistants—all contributed to every step of the University's progress.' "

In the first years of the Evening Institute, Dr. Speare initiated many classes, courses, and groups of courses. Some of his plans failed to materialize. On one occasion he visited a class in bookkeeping to enlist students for a course in Knots and Splices, because as an ardent yachtsman and with a retired sea captain available as teacher he believed the course would be valuable and appealing; according to the memory of a member of the bookkeeping class, there were no recruits for the new course.

Some of the courses and "schools" were temporary, but all of them were motivated by Dr. Speare's desire to promote and develop educational opportunities for young men who would otherwise have few or none.

Many of the projects were independent, imaginative experiments. At the "Evening Institute Spread" of 1906 a speaker

Frank Palmer Speare

said, "Ten years ago Mr. Speare was the only man who dared dream of such wild schemes as special schools. Today special schools are found in all our larger cities with wide-awake Associations, successfully conducted under their auspices."

Dr. Speare was essentially a man of ideas and expansive forward view, for the record shows that often when a new enterprise was underway to the point of giving reasonable promise of permanence, he lost interest in it and began thinking of other possibilities.

Abundant energy and varied interests are reflected by the fact that for a long time Dr. Speare was an active and admired public speaker. He traveled frequently on speaking engagements and in later years was fond of saying that time was when the best known names in New England were those of Lydia Pinkham and Frank Palmer Speare. The titles of some speeches indicate themes which were developed with lightness and good humor, unusual fluency of language, but with positive, constructive emphasis: "Enduring Satisfactions," "Building a Career," "The High Cost of Ignorance," "The Man Who Arrives."

Dr. Speare had perception in seeing the possibilities in other men, and the wisdom to give those possibilities full freedom to develop. As a small college became a complex university, he delegated increasing responsibility to others in the organization. In 1925 the structure of Northeastern was revised by the creation of two posts of vice president, one occupied by Dr. Ell, in charge of the Day Division; the other by Dr. Churchill, in charge of the Evening Division. Thereafter, the two vice presidents directed the procedure and details of the actual operation of the University.

One of the many evidences of Dr. Speare's foresight, and his willingness to let others develop the work which he had started, is a "Professional Will and Codicil," written in 1937 and filed with the Board of Trustees through the chairman, Mr. Dodge. Dr. Speare wrote, "I am now in my sixty-eighth year and have always contemplated retiring at seventy and shall be glad to do so if it would be of benefit to Northeastern."

A final section of the "will" reflects the idealism and unselfish interest which carried Dr. Speare through his long period of diligent work as an educator:

"The dominating motive in my life has been the establishment and perpetuation of this great People's University. I have put everything that I possessed into it and it is fulfilling its function magnificently.

"I can retire from the Presidency with confidence as to its future, based upon the devotion of its loyal, sympathetic trustees, and its skilled executive staff and faculties.

"It has been a great privilege to serve the state and city of my birth in this way and I take this opportunity of expressing my profound appreciation for the wonderful support given me by the officers and directors of the Boston Y.M.C.A., the officers and trustees and faculty of Northeastern University, and the tens of thousands of alumni who are living examples of the ennobling influences emanating from Northeastern."

In 1941, his first year as President Emeritus of Northeastern University, Dr. Speare received his third honorary LL.D. degree. The others had been from Northeastern and the University of New Hampshire. The third was from Harvard University, with the citation: "Frank Palmer Speare—First President of Northeastern University, builder of our newest academic neighbor; the college of Henry Dunster congratulates a founding father."

Until a final illness, Dr. Speare continued to be vigorous and active after his retirement from Northeastern. In letters he referred to "getting my new office (at the Chandler School) in condition." And "from present indications, I am going to have many opportunities for useful service." His feeling of identity with Northeastern shows in the statement, soon after his leaving the presidency, "I am purchasing several pairs of new shoes because I find my old ones take me up Huntington Avenue, in spite of all I can do."

As Director of the Evening Institute, and President of Northeastern College and of Northeastern University, Dr. Speare was a pioneer, an inspiration, a directive force, and the man who laid foundations on which others made developments with further creativity.

Galen David Light

Mr. Light joined the staff of the Boston YMCA in 1901 at the age of twenty-four, and retired from the position of Secretary and Treasurer of Northeastern University in 1943.

During that span of time, Mr. Light occupied many positions. He was Assistant Educational Director, working with Mr. Speare in the early years of the Evening Institute. He was Secretary of the Executive Council of Northeastern College when it was formed in 1916. Along the way, he had been Registrar, and for a year Superintendent of both the Automobile School and the School of Applied Electricity. He held numerous other titles; Mr. Light himself has said that in the formative period of changing schools and personnel, his name was listed whenever a vacancy in the roster needed to be filled. His major service in later years was as Secretary of the College and then the University, Secretary of the Board of Trustees, and Treasurer of the University.

To all of these positions Mr. Light brought assets that grew from ability, preparation, and temperament.

Born in Pennsylvania, Mr. Light moved from a country setting to earn both a B.S. and an A.B. at Lebanon Valley College. Then he went to Yale and received another A.B. in 1901. By that time he was interested in the work of the YMCA, because of student participation at Lebanon Valley College and Yale. His interest stemmed, also, from a family background which had developed in him a strong sense of personal integrity and a concern for other people.

High standards were a handicap in Mr. Light's college years. To keep himself in college he worked at night for a druggist who, in the easygoing manner of the time, filled all prescriptions, including those for drugs and alcohol, which bore a doctor's signature. Accommodating doctors were always available, but Mr. Light disliked filling "Sunday prescriptions" which were legally valid but morally illicit. The druggist solved the problem by having his wife fill such prescriptions when the student assistant was on duty.

Working his way through college prepared Mr. Light for the demanding job he assumed with the Boston YMCA, on duty three evenings a week at the start, and increasingly through the years carrying positions in which he was held responsible for accounts and reports that involved detailed work and meticulous accuracy.

By temperament Mr. Light was well suited to fit into the pattern of the men who built Northeastern. In matters of planning and policy he was a needed conservative, often striking a balance in discussions in which differing opinions and objectives caused tension. Because of his precision, accuracy, and stout qualities of honesty, Mr. Light was universally liked and respected.

As stated by a Northeastern teacher and administrator who has known Mr. Light well for over thirty years:

"Galen D. Light gave to his long years of service to Northeastern such soundness of moral character that his name among us instantly links itself with such attributes as honor, straightforwardness, and fine decency.

"Yet with all his firm rectitude there was warm understanding and kindliness. His quiet sense of humor and even temper mellowed his unyielding integrity. While he had a reputation for exactness and thoroughness in all matters of statistics and records, his chief concern centered in human values and in persons as such. Though he was not given to much talk about it, a deeply religious spirit permeated his daily life among us. It was this spirit which enabled him to combine humility with self-confidence, gentleness with moral courage, magnanimity toward others with strong convictions within himself."

Another summary of Mr. Light's contribution to Northeast-

Galen David Light

ern is the following resolution, incorporated in the permanent records of the University:

"RESOLVED: That the Board of Trustees express to Galen David Light, who will retire from active duty on June 30, 1943, its sincere appreciation for his faithful, loyal, and unremitting service to Northeastern University.

"Appointed to the staff in 1901, Mr. Light occupied successively several positions of responsibility. His most noteworthy service has been as Secretary and Treasurer of the University, having occupied the former position for the past twenty-seven years and the latter for the past eleven years, prior to which he was Comptroller. In recent years he has also been a member of the Corporation and the Board of Trustees. The responsibilities of these highly important positions he has discharged ably and well. He has indeed contributed in a signal manner to the development of the University from the early beginning of its educational programs to the present time.

"The Board of Trustees extends to Mr. Light its sincere hope that he may have the utmost happiness in whatever he may undertake in the future."

Carl Stephens Ell

The second President of Northeastern, in the later years of his own term of office, which extended from 1940 to 1959, was introduced at public occasions and often referred to privately as "Mr. Northeastern." The reason was that during his presidency and even before that time he was the central force which made possible the building of a university, in terms of campus and structures; growth in colleges, numbers of students, and corresponding educational status; and major and minor innovations within the university which even now have become traditional.

Dr. Ell started life in Indiana, a member of a third generation of a German family which originally had come to this country by way of Boston but had moved on to the open farm-

43

ing area of the Middle West. From the farm he went to DePauw Academy and then to the Methodist university of the same name, where he completed four years' work in three while he supported himself by jobs at manual labor in free time. During those years, as one writer about Dr. Ell has said, "He learned to make every motion count; he trained himself to know the essential from the nonessential."

In 1909, Dr. Ell came east to do graduate study at M.I.T., with a view to a life work in civil engineering. In the following year another of those coincidences of time, place, and people occurred. Dr. Ell says,

"Early in the fall of 1910, Professor Howard in the Surveying Department asked me if I would teach a course in surveying at the YMCA. Since I was earning my way through M.I.T. (and being bold, if not discreet), I said that Barkus was willing to try.

"At that time, the classes were being conducted in an old, rambling frame dwelling, located on the exact spot where the Boston City Club was later built and which came to be known as the Mason Building.

"On or about October 1, 1910, I went to the YMCA and talked with the Educational Director, Frank Palmer Speare, about the program. I began teaching the eight students of the first day class in surveying, which later turned out to be the first class in Civil Engineering in what is now the College of Engineering."

The limitations and by later standards the primitive conditions of the first years of co-operative engineering education in Boston are recreated by Dr. Ell's recall of the conditions under which he worked as an instructor.

"The class work was conducted in the attic of the building, where we frequently banged our heads against the rafters as we straightened up from the drawing table.

"The YMCA had no Civil Engineering equipment, so it was necessary to take the small class of four or five students down to 387 Washington Street where the B. L. Makepeace Company

Carl Stephens Ell

was located, rent a transit, level, or other equipment such as surveying rods, tapes and chains, at the rate of $1.50 for the afternoon, then proceed up Winter Street to the Common, where we had our field work and surveying exercises around the Frog Pond. After the field exercise was completed, the class returned the equipment to the Makepeace Company and signed off for the day."

In 1912, having received his Master of Science degree from M.I.T., Dr. Ell became one of the seven members of the teaching staff of the YMCA Co-operative School of Engineering. Two years later he was made Assistant Dean of the school and in 1917 succeeded Hercules Geromanos as Dean.

By that time the major programs of the YMCA Evening Institute had become Northeastern College of the Boston Young Men's Christian Association, with the Co-operative School of Engineering as the most conspicuous and promising unit.

During a period extending over nearly fifty years, Dr. Ell devoted himself exclusively to the development of Northeastern. Since that period comes down to the present time, it is still too early to see all of the elements in final perspective and relationship. Yet some central facts and conclusions are clear.

Dr. Ell has always been a hard worker. Mr. Light, in commenting on the early years, said, "He was tremendously active, carrying a heavy schedule both day and evening, and never seeming tired." That energy continued, and accounted for the cumulative accomplishment.

As Dean, Vice President, and President, Dr. Ell expected hard work from others. A common comment on a special assignment was, "Take as much time as you want, so long as the job is done by nine o'clock tomorrow morning." Repeatedly he pointed out to his faculty that a job at Northeastern was a twenty-four-hour-a-day job, and while few if any in the organization came as near the maximum as Dr. Ell himself did, many people worked long hours, carrying heavy teaching schedules and additional responsibilities. Inevitably there was grumbling and self-pity, yet a surprising number of teachers, administrators, and office workers stayed on through the years, experiencing good times and bad, depressions and wars alternating with periods of prosperity as an unendowed university operated on a balanced annual budget.

Workers at Northeastern caught from Dr. Ell the feeling that they were a part of a growing institution which already was performing a valuable service to youth and which had unlimited possibilities. The present might be arduous, but the future offered promise.

A distinguished teacher and thinker left a small conventional New England college to join the faculty of a new university in the Boston area during its early uncertain years. His explanation was, "After fourteen years, I found that everything was predictable. There was no surprise element of stimulation in students, administration, or the total future of the college." At Northeastern, everything was unpredictable from year to year, and the surprises were many. The number of people who have spent their entire professional lives at Northeastern demonstrates that along with uncertainty and surprises there was also current reward, and faith in the future.

The establishment of the Northeastern home was a long and difficult process. Although the buildings which have been referred to as "the miracle on Huntington Avenue" are the result of interest and assistance by thousands of persons, with the development plan initiated during the administration of President Speare, for many years the direction and execution of the plan was centered in the initiative and work of Dr. Ell.

Less apparent than buildings are the internal advances, improvements, and refinements which have been incorporated in the growth of Northeastern during the past twenty years. Directly or indirectly all of these changes stem from the ideas, plans, and desires of the second President.

The widening circle of friends and financial contributors, the development of the University Corporation, the establishment of the Permanent Faculty and other personnel groups, and the initiation of annual events involving faculty, students, alumni, staff, Corporation members, and visitors represent a broadening basis of activity which has resulted in an increased sense of identity with Northeastern in those participating. These and other contributions to the permanence of Northeastern will appear at many points in the following record.

Recognition of Dr. Ell's accomplishment has come to him from many quarters. Since 1935, honorary degrees have been conferred by DePauw University, Tufts University, Boston University, University of Rhode Island, Emerson College, and Northeastern University. In 1957 at DePauw, Dr. Ell was recipient of "The Old Gold Goblet," given annually by vote of the senior class to an outstanding alumnus of the University.

In October of 1958 a dinner of eight hundred members of the extensive Northeastern family signalized Dr. Ell's retirement from the Presidency of the University. Dr. Russell J. Humbert, President of DePauw University, spoke on "DePauw Salutes a Distinguished Son." Mr. Dodge announced the renaming of the Student Center Building as the "Carl Stephens Ell Student Center." This permanent tribute had been promoted by Michael T. Kelleher, an active member of the Corporation and Board of Trustees, who frequently introduced Dr. Ell at meetings as "my favorite college president"; a distinct loss to Northeastern, as to the Commonwealth, was Mr. Kelleher's death only nine days after the October dinner.

It is too early to summarize and evaluate Dr. Ell's contribution to Northeastern, both because of the immediacy of time and perspective and because that contribution is still in progress, even though Dr. Ell is now President Emeritus. It is clear, however, that Northeastern University as a major university, permanently established physically and educationally, owes more to Dr. Ell than to any other single person of the large group who have aided in that development.

Origin and Development of Northeastern University

Everett Avery Churchill

The fourth member of the central core of those who determined the structure and future of Northeastern is another man who devoted his life to that one area of work.

Dr. Speare had held other positions before he joined the staff of the YMCA, and in later years he carried on additional activities, but his primary interest and concern was the Evening Institute and the developments that came from it. Mr. Light and Dr. Ell entered the educational work of the YMCA as young men and stayed on permanently. Similarly, Dr. Churchill devoted a full and productive professional life to one institution.

Dr. Churchill's educational preparation was varied, and spread over a ten-year period. After his graduation from Bridgewater Normal School in 1914, he went on to Wesleyan University to receive an A.B. degree, magna cum laude. In 1921 he received an Ed.M. degree from Harvard University and three years later, also from Harvard, the degree of Ed.D.

In the interval of interrupted education Dr. Churchill did World War I service as a commissioned officer, and in 1919 came to Boston to join the faculty of The Huntington School. The following year he became Dean of the Law School, and thereafter was an integral part of the central personnel which planned and developed Northeastern University.

From 1922 to 1925, Dr. Churchill carried, along with his other titles, that of "Unit Director." In that capacity he supervised the Northeastern evening programs in Worcester, Springfield, Providence, New Haven, and Bridgeport. He developed and implemented an elaborate and exact system of inspection and reports, in an effort to insure quality standards in the work conducted by these outlying units of the Northeastern system.

As Vice President, in 1925, Dr. Churchill was in charge of the Evening Division, and guided it through a difficult period of adjustment, as changing local and world conditions resulted in new concepts, standards, and objectives for all evening edu-

50

Everett Avery Churchill

cation, including that at Northeastern. By supervising teachers and administrators during this period, and by bringing to bear upon the structure and conduct of schools and curricula his technical knowledge and philosophy of education, Dr. Churchill laid the foundations on which later developments, especially those following World War II, were built.

When Mr. Light retired in 1943, Dr. Churchill became Secretary of the Northeastern University Corporation. At the same time he took over responsibility for University budgets and finances, and for supervision of "grounds and buildings."

The last two of these three phases of his position as Vice President became increasingly complex during the next ten years.

After the lean period of World War II, finances of income and expenditure, gifts, scholarships, and other special funds expanded rapidly. Dr. Churchill planned an intricate network of day and evening budgets, and saw to it that forecasts and commitments were adhered to.

"Grounds and buildings" grew even more vigorously. The Student Center and the Library were built, and Dr. Churchill acted as University representative in negotiating contracts and supervising details of construction as the contracts were fulfilled. The legal technicalities of the purchase of additional land and the problems of maintenance, improvement, and remodeling of an expanding educational plant were also parts of Dr. Churchill's work; in the latter area he was ably assisted by J. Kenneth Stevenson, Supervisor of Grounds and Buildings, who worked closely with Dr. Churchill as both administrator and friend.

To all of these kinds of work Dr. Churchill brought a scholarly mind, precise and disciplined, trained to reduce to essentials either a mass of statistical data or a voluminous governmental report. Like many others of Northeastern's personnel through the decades, his first concern was doing the job well and getting it done, whether the time required ended at five o'clock, or late in the evening, or during the weekend. He was always up to date in his work, and at the same time planning for the future.

In 1953, ill health forced Dr. Churchill to retire from active work at Northeastern. Until his death in December, 1959, he followed from a distance the progress of Northeastern, and maintained the interest which motivated him during thirty-four years of personal participation.

The personality and individual qualities of Dr. Churchill, different from those of the other major administrators in the formative period of Northeastern, are well summarized by one who knew him well during his term as Vice President:

"I am certain that in the historical account of every progressive educational institution in this country there will be found a section devoted to Dr. Churchill—one of the Dr. Churchills of education. These are the men who served ably in the early days of growth, at Northeastern and elsewhere, who worked long hours, expended wisely, conserved assets, and urged their associates to greater accomplishment in order that the institution they worked for might prosper and grow. Such was Northeastern's Dr. Churchill.

"It was my privilege to know Dr. Churchill over an extended period of time. He was short of stature, rather rotund, energetic, and that rare combination of scholar, gentleman, and astute administrator. He was a strict disciplinarian in all matters pertaining to the financial structure and operation of the University. Especially in periods of financial stress and strain, woe unto the department head who exceeded his budget!

"Often Dr. Churchill, engrossed in the effort to solve a University problem, has walked past me without speaking, but several hours later has called me by my first name, and settled down to chat about the recent performance of a particular racing yacht, the art of boxing (and on one occasion he demonstrated the 'right cross' so effectively that I found myself flattened against a nearby wall), or the reason why the Boston Red Sox Club was in fourth place instead of at the top of the league. Then the talk might turn to books, theories of education, international relations—anything. The versatility of Dr. Churchill's interests and detailed knowledge was unusual, refreshing, and stimulating.

"It was not given to Dr. Churchill to have intimate contact with the Northeastern student body, or with many of the faculty, for the very nature of his work precluded this relationship. Any student or faculty member would have gained much from knowing Dr. Churchill.

"As is often the case in the affairs of men, fate in the form of a disabling illness forced Dr. Churchill to retire prematurely. Thus was closed the active career of a man who was respected greatly by all who knew him, for his accomplishments, his devotion to duty, and his vigorous, unpredictable responses to life and all that it contains."

The University Pattern

Under the guidance of these four men—Dr. Speare, Dr. Ell, Dr. Churchill, and Mr. Light—and with other men and women performing valuable services at many major and minor points, Northeastern evolved a pattern of education which met community needs and at the same time proved to be efficient and economical for an institution which was making its own independent way.

Evening education for employed adults continued to be an inherent part of the Northeastern plan. The Law School, the School of Commerce and Finance, and the Polytechnic School were administered and directed by Northeastern College after the college was formed. The last two, under the names "School of Business" and "Lincoln Institute" became important schools in the Evening Division which developed from 1945 onward. Throughout the years—in YMCA buildings, in rented quarters, and later in the University's own buildings—evening schools made possible a double use of classrooms and other areas, and to a certain extent personnel and equipment. At the same time, they carried on the original purpose and intention of the Evening Institute.

Co-operative education proved to be sound and successful. The School of Engineering grew slowly but steadily for some years and after 1917 moved into a period of increasing size and significance. Three other day colleges were added.

The College of Business Administration, established in 1922 with Turner F. Garner as its first Dean, operated as a full-time school for four years and then adopted the Co-operative Plan.

In 1935 a co-operative College of Liberal Arts started its first year with an enrollment of thirty-five. At that time co-operative education in the liberal arts areas of sciences and the humanities had been attempted by few institutions. Antioch College had been operating its program, completely in liberal arts, since 1921. Four other colleges were conducting co-operative education in science and applied arts. Again, Northeastern was experimental. The College of Liberal Arts developed, however, and by 1941 was a substantial unit in the University group.

The fourth college, the College of Education, established in 1953, completed the structure of the Day Division. This college began as a four-year full-time school of education; in its third year, it instituted a teacher-internship program, with the result that it became a co-operative school.

Early in its development, Northeastern was committed to "co-operative education by day, adult education in the evening." The combination made it an unusual university—a pioneer in adult education, and the only institution in New England to operate all of its day colleges on the principles and application of co-operative education.

This permanent pattern enabled the University to broaden and intensify its inherited function of supplementing the educational opportunities available in the Boston area, at the same time providing some new and different opportunities.

V

ESTABLISHING AN INDEPENDENT
UNIVERSITY

On March 30, 1916, the Secretary of the Commonwealth
signed a bill, already passed by the General Court, which
created Northeastern College "for the purpose of furnishing
instruction and teaching in all branches of education in connection with the Boston Y.M.C.A. and to do any and all things
connected with or incidental to the purposes of its organization."

Northeastern College of the Boston Young Men's Christian
Association was a legal corporation, and a basis for educational
administration. The members of the corporate body were
Arthur S. Johnson, Lewis A. Crossett, George W. Brainard,
Charles W. Perkins, H. Bradlee Fenno, Sabin P. Sanger, William E. Murdock, Frank P. Speare, and George W. Mehaffey.
To them and to their associates and successors were assigned
by law "powers, rights, and privileges," but "subject to the
limitations, duties and restrictions, which by law appertain
thereto."

The structure of the college was a Board of Trustees, headed
by Arthur S. Johnson, President of the Boston YMCA; and an
Executive Council, made up of Frank Palmer Speare as President; Galen D. Light, Secretary; and the deans of the schools.

The new college had, within its own rights and privileges,
no degree-granting power. It undertook the conduct of a group
of day and evening schools. According to a public announce-

ment in March of 1916, the name "Northeastern College" would be applied to the Evening Law School, the School of Commerce and Finance, the Co-operative Engineering School, the Polytechnic School, and a new and short-lived School of Liberal Arts. Affiliated schools were the School of Business, the evening Preparatory School, The Huntington School, and the Automobile School.

Two legislative acts of incorporation had preceded the formation of Northeastern College.

In 1904 the Evening Law School of the Boston Young Men's Christian Association was incorporated by action of the General Court, and given power to grant the degree of bachelor of laws. The original members of the corporation were James R. Dunbar, James B. Ames, Samuel C. Bennett, D. Chauncey Brewer, Josiah H. Quincy, Francis B. Sears, and George W. Mehaffey; a section of the legislative act provided that the body should always consist of seven members, of whom four should be members of the Board of Directors of the Boston YMCA.

In 1910 the School of Commerce and Finance of the Boston Young Men's Christian Association was incorporated, and in the following year by a separate act was authorized to confer the degrees of Bachelor of Commercial Science and Master of Commercial Science "appropriate to the courses of study offered in accordance with the provisions of its charter."

For several years after 1916, Northeastern College functioned as a governing and directive organization. Technically it was the Educational Department of the Boston YMCA, but as the college developed, its component parts came to have identity of their own. For example, the names of the two degree-granting schools were changed to "Northeastern College, School of Law of the Boston Young Men's Christian Association" and "Northeastern College, School of Commerce and Finance of the Boston Young Men's Christian Association," and thereafter degrees were issued under those names.

On March 17, 1920, a legislative act, carrying among other signatures that of the then Governor, Calvin Coolidge, gave

Establishing an Independent University

Northeastern College authorization to grant bachelor's degrees in civil, mechanical, chemical, and electrical engineering. These degrees were applicable to the Co-operative School of Engineering, which by 1920 had recovered from the World War I interim and under the direction of Dean Ell was developing rapidly, not only in numbers but in quality of both academic work and co-operative employment.

Following the passage of the bill, a "Degree Jubilee," organized by Professor Joseph Spear, was held at the college, with students and faculty celebrating the new status of their college as an institution of legally recognized academic standing.

At the June commencement of 1920, seventy-six engineering degrees were awarded, forty of them to alumni who had qualified under the requirements of the legislative act.

The year 1922 is another decisive one in the history of Northeastern. In March, the name of the institution was changed from "College" to "University." Within the same year, Robert G. Dodge, F. R. Carnegie Steele, and Walton I. Crocker were elected to the Board of Trustees; they were the first Trustees who were not at the same time Directors of the Boston YMCA.

The next twenty-six years constitute a slow and at some points painful process of determining and establishing the identity and autonomy of Northeastern.

Equally important was the preparation of Northeastern schools and curricula for acceptance by professional and academic bodies. That accreditation came later, from such organizations as the University of the State of New York, the Engineers' Council for Professional Development, and the New England Association of Colleges and Secondary Schools.

Numerical growth accelerated steadily and during some periods rapidly from 1922 onward, and whereas physical space for educational work had been a problem in the early 1900's, by 1930 the need for Northeastern buildings was not only evident but imperative. Evident, also, was the inescapable fact that no institution can plan and live its own life as a part of another institution.

While Northeastern grew in other respects, it moved, by successive steps, toward freedom of action and the determination of its future. In 1924 the financial accounts of the University and the Boston YMCA were separated, thereby absolving the YMCA from further financial responsibility and enabling the University to plan and administer its own funds. In 1932 Mr. Dodge was elected Chairman of the Board of Trustees, the first Chairman not from the YMCA organization; his immediate predecessor was T. Grafton Abbott, President of the Boston YMCA. Other changes were made from time to time in the constituency of the Board of Trustees, varying the proportion of YMCA and non-YMCA members.

It soon became apparent that the young University was more than a Department of Education, as that term was then used in other Young Men's Christian Associations, and in similar organizations. At the same time, the Boston YMCA regarded Northeastern as a part of its structure, since it had founded the first unit of the institution in 1898 and, directly or indirectly, had made possible the developments which followed that date.

The gradual and eventually the complete separation of Northeastern from the Boston YMCA was the result of two parallel lines of change: the expansion of an educational institution, and the corresponding necessity for that institution to determine and direct its own expansion.

Northeastern University as a legal entity made steady improvement. It obtained the right to increase the amount of property which it might hold. In 1923 it was authorized by the General Court "to confer such degrees as are usually conferred by colleges and universities in this commonwealth, except medical and dental degrees and degrees of bachelor of science and bachelor of arts." In 1930 a legislative act added the B.S. with specifications, and in 1935 a final authorization empowered Northeastern "to confer such degrees as are usually conferred by colleges and universities in this commonwealth, but excepting medical and dental degrees."

This extension of degree-granting power was the result of

both internal and external efforts, involving the solution of immediate problems, long-range planning, careful educational and financial administration, and the enlistment of public support and recognition. The central figures in this detailed, arduous, and often discouraging program were Dr. Ell and Dr. Churchill.

An objective view of the relationship between Northeastern and the Boston YMCA was provided by the John Price Jones Corporation report to the Northeastern Board of Trustees in July of 1931. This report, of nearly three hundred pages, presented a detailed analysis of the University, an estimate of its possibilities of future development and service, and a proposed plan for raising money for buildings and endowment.

Among the "suggestions regarding future organization of the University" was the recommendation that the Bylaws be changed to provide a Board of Trustees of forty-five, with the stipulation that "Board members who are also Directors of the Boston YMCA shall at no time constitute a majority of the membership."

The reasons given for this recommendation are: "We foresee difficulty in attracting to the University Board men of influence and vision, outside of the Y.M.C.A. Directors, while such men have no actual control, in the last analysis, of the University's management and policies." And "Without an autonomous Board there would be difficulty in interesting large givers, particularly the Foundations and higher education 'philanthropists' of the country. Persons of large means might properly hesitate to give to an institution whose control lies with another organization founded primarily for other than educational purposes."

Through the 1930's the leaders of both the YMCA and the University worked on the tenuous problem of relationship between the two institutions.

In 1935, an organization chart, prepared by Dr. Churchill and accepted as at least a temporary basis of operation, shows an interlocking and overlapping directorate, with ten members serving concurrently on the YMCA Board of Directors and the Board of Trustees of the University.

A year later the Bylaws of the University were amended to provide for the formation of a Corporation of seventy-five members, with a Board of Trustees to be elected from and by its membership, and four standing committees: Executive, Development, Funds and Investments, and Housing.

The formal organization of the Northeastern University Corporation, the most important single event in the evolution of Northeastern's structure, took place on January 22, 1937, at a dinner meeting at which James L. Richards was host and chairman. Speakers on the past, present, and future of the University were Robert G. Dodge, President Speare, Vice Presidents Ell and Churchill, and Frank L. Richardson, Vice Chairman of the Corporation and Chairman of the Development Committee.

The Corporation as then established consisted of seventy-four members, with Mr. Dodge as Chairman and Mr. Light as Secretary. Within the Corporation a Board of Trustees of thirty-one, including eight Directors of the Boston YMCA, was elected. The Corporation thus became the controlling body of Northeastern University.

Incidental changes, matters of legality and technicality, were made at other points along the way. In 1935 the words "of the Boston Young Men's Christian Association" were eliminated from the corporate name "Northeastern University." In 1947 the purpose of the Northeastern University Corporation was simplified to the statement: "for the purpose of providing instruction in any or all branches of education and doing anything incidental thereto." Finally, in 1948, a revision of the Charter and Bylaws made Northeastern completely independent in all respects.

Like other phases of the history of the University, autonomy and self-sufficiency were the products of an evolutionary growth, and of a progress that was inevitable, in view of the leadership which Northeastern has had.

VI

ADAPTATION TO CHANGE

In the minutes of the meeting of the Board of Trustees on April 10, 1953, appears the record:

"It was voted that the educational policy of Northeastern University be stated as follows:

"Northeastern University is a community service institution which seeks to discover and to meet important needs in the field of higher education. Its offerings are designed to serve substantial groups of students in programs for which there is genuine demand and which are not adequately provided by other colleges and universities in the Boston area.

"The University does not conceive its function to include the committing of institutional resources for the purpose of carrying on schools, curricula, or courses that serve the needs of very few students at high expense or that duplicate unnecessarily the opportunities available at neighboring institutions.

"Northeastern tries to apply its energies and facilities to educational enterprises that will yield maximum advantages to the community. The University is primarily concerned with teaching at the undergraduate and graduate levels and limits its activities in research to those which will be stimulating and helpful to the faculty as means toward the enhancement of instruction."

This statement is a formal summary of educational principle, thinking, and planning inherent in the history of Northeastern.

Few universities have been so flexible, even during the first half of the twentieth century, when many American colleges and universities chose or were forced to modify curricula, schools, and even basic structure.

In the early years, the YMCA work in education was fluid as well as flexible. After the formation of Northeastern College, the basic policy was one of planned adaptation to changing interests and desires on the part of young people, and changing needs and requirements of a new century. The result was frequent adjustment of educational programs, balanced with the maintenance and expansion of a self-sustaining, operative university.

Ten decisive structural changes, occurring in the period from the 1920's to the 1950's, illustrate the background to and the implementation of the statement by the Board of Trustees in 1953.

(1) The Automobile School was from 1903 a part of the Department of Education of the Boston YMCA, and later a school affiliated with Northeastern. By the mid-1920's the automobile had become an accepted ingredient of the times; it was no longer an experiment, or a mysterious marvel, or the rich man's toy. The personnel of the Automobile School had therefore changed, as conditions changed.

In 1926 it was evident that the school had served its purpose. It was discontinued for that reason, and because the areas it occupied in the present Botolph Building, then the Vocational Building, were needed for the work of the School of Engineering.

(2) Outlying branches of Northeastern work had been established and developed in the period 1917 to 1920, beginning with evening law work in Worcester and extending to additional schools in Springfield, Providence, New Haven, and Bridgeport. These schools conducted some college preparatory work and some technical courses, but mainly study in law and business, leading to Northeastern degrees. The schools were

supervised by a special committee under the direction of Dr. Churchill.

As Northeastern concentrated its efforts in Boston and as some of the branches built up a basis for their own identity, the University withdrew from responsibility in other cities, starting with the Bridgeport branch in 1924, and completing the disassociation in Springfield in 1951.

Three present-day institutions are outgrowths of Northeastern branches. They are Worcester Junior College; Western New England College, Springfield; Roger Williams Junior College, Providence; and Bridgeport Engineering Institute, which in 1924 took over the Northeastern technical courses and developed an independent and successful school of engineering.

(3) The College of Liberal Arts, established in 1935, was an effort to offer the educational and financial advantages of the Co-operative Plan to students in non-technical areas of study and in the humanities. It has increased in size, slowly but substantially, and has proved its effectiveness as preparation for careers directly upon graduation and for advanced study in graduate schools.

Co-operative work assignments for Liberal Arts students have necessarily proved difficult, especially in periods of economic lag. For students majoring in mathematics, physics, chemistry, and biology, jobs which correlate classroom study with field experience present no real problem. For students majoring in history, government, English, and modern languages, however, work which combines monetary and educational advantage to the student is not easy to locate and supervise. Yet the record of employment and the personal values which students have derived from co-operative work experience have justified the original and sustained effort. Moreover, the College of Liberal Arts, under the direction of Dean Wilfred Lake, has established both status and accomplishment in preparing students for graduate work.

(4) Northeastern's inherited tradition was education for

young men, but this masculine emphasis was modified as time passed. There was, in fact, historical precedent for co-education in the Northeastern system, going back to the pre-Evening Institute period. Dr. Churchill, in his *History of Northeastern University 1896–1927*, wrote, "In 1891 and 1892 we find that women were no longer admitted to the evening classes, on the grounds that there was not adequate room to accommodate even the men who applied for admission to courses."

Co-education was adopted by different schools for varying reasons and over a long period of time. Some of the early courses in the Automobile School were open to ladies, and during World War I there were special courses for women drivers; no records are available, however, to indicate how many ladies took advantage of these opportunities. The School of Law admitted women students in 1922. In the same year the School of Commerce and Finance became co-educational, and in 1926 granted six degrees, including one Master of Commercial Science degree, to women. The Preparatory School accepted women students in 1925, and later, when the Preparatory School had become Lincoln Preparatory School, it appealed particularly to young women who needed academic credit in preparation for nurses' training.

In 1943, the colleges of the Day Division adopted co-education. Six women students entered Northeastern that year: four in Liberal Arts, and one each in Engineering and Business Administration. Four of this pioneer group on the Co-operative Plan completed their five-year courses and received degrees.

An Adviser to Women was appointed, and in 1954 the title was changed to Dean of Women; that position was first held by Dr. Myra Herrick, who had been Adviser to Women for four years.

The first Northeastern daughter was Marjorie Faunce, Liberal Arts 1949, whose father, Laurence S. Faunce, was of the Engineering class of 1922. Miss Faunce married George Brumis, Class of 1945.

From 1943 on, women students have constituted a proportionately small but important part of the student body of the co-operative colleges, largest in numbers in the College of Liberal Arts, and in recent years, in the College of Education.

(5) By 1950, the size and complexity of undergraduate programs at Northeastern and the beginnings of graduate work gave evidence that the University could not function effectively with affiliated secondary and college preparatory work. The Huntington School was therefore disassociated from the Northeastern structure, and became a part of the Boston YMCA, where it had had its origin.

(6) The announcement of the closing of the School of Law in 1953, and the completion of its work in 1956 was a conspicuous step in the process of adaptation.

As the first unit in the Northeastern system, the Law School had built up a sound record and reputation over a period of fifty-five years. The conditions and need which had brought the school into being, however, had changed greatly with the passing of a half-century. Moreover, requirements by accrediting bodies of the legal profession made an evening law school with a small day program difficult to administer at the level of standards which had been established in previous decades.

A view of the closing of the Law School, as stated editorially by the Boston *Globe* in April of 1953, shows perhaps the weight of more objective judgment than was easy to see in 1953:

"The decision of Northeastern University to close its Law School will doubtless jolt its many law alumni. Yet the attitude displayed by the University authorities in making this move will doubtless win their approval and that of the community Northeastern serves, when the matter is weighed carefully.

"What Northeastern is doing, in fact, is shifting its educational energies to fields where the need is greater than it is for turning out law graduates. As the University officials truly state, facilities exist elsewhere in sufficient quantity and quality already, in the matter of law schools. Other fields are not so amply served. To serve them better is sound policy.

"Northeastern has long since established itself as an institute whose policies connote courage, wise perception of social, economic, and scientific trends, and a determination to serve the community through close co-operation. Its latest decision cleaves to that ideal."

(7) The "shifting of energies" at Northeastern was demonstrated by the establishment of the College of Education for the academic year 1953–1954.

The need for more elementary and secondary school teachers, and the prospect of a cumulative need in the on-coming decade, were the subject of many ominous conclusions and predictions, both locally and nationally, in the early 1950's. A survey of teacher-training opportunities in Greater Boston indicated that a school of education which emphasized subject matter and teachable course content in major fields of specialization, as well as including technical courses in education as a science and an art, would serve a constructive purpose.

The College of Education, under the deanship of Dr. Lester Vander Werf, who came to Northeastern from the University of New Hampshire, started its first year, offering both undergraduate and graduate curricula. It has continued that combination, with the addition of the Teacher Internship Plan.

(8) Evening courses to prepare students for entrance to college constitute another of the fifty-year projects at Northeastern.

The Evening Preparatory School was started in 1904, as a part of the YMCA Evening Institute. In 1927 it became Lincoln Preparatory School, affiliated with Northeastern University, and with James W. Lees as its Principal. Thereafter it grew in enrollment and extent of curriculum as it met the needs of young men, and in later years young women who had been unable to complete their high school years or who needed particular courses to fulfill the requirements for entrance to college.

In its most active period, the 1940's, when Donald H. MacKenzie was directing the school, Lincoln School offered a complete preparatory curriculum: physics, chemistry, biology, mathematics, English, economics, government, French, Latin,

Spanish, German. During that period it was the only preparatory school in the Boston area offering such a diversity of evening courses.

After World War II, the function which Lincoln School had performed was no longer a real need, mainly because of comprehensive examinations instituted and conducted by the Massachusetts Department of Education to provide students with substantial credit toward a high school diploma. Consequently, Lincoln Preparatory School was discontinued in 1954, although some of its courses in mathematics and science were carried on for two years thereafter by Lincoln Institute to complete the work which students had started in the preparatory school.

(9) The elimination of college preparatory work from the Northeastern structure was accounted for in large measure by a recognition of other educational areas in which the University was prepared to do more valuable work than it could do at the secondary level. Increasing specialization and the extension of boundaries in all scientific fields demonstrated a new need for more people trained in advanced academic study. Consequently, Northeastern, which had deliberately limited itself to undergraduate programs, added graduate study to its basic structure and function. As with other movements toward adaptation, the addition was a process of successive steps.

In 1940 teaching fellows were accepted by the Department of Chemistry of the College of Liberal Arts, to receive a Master's degree after two years of seminar courses, directed research, and teaching in the form of laboratory supervision. This common American pattern of graduate work was later used by the Department of Biology and the Department of Physics, and in the College of Business Administration by the Department of Accounting. After the establishment of the Graduate School in 1958, it was extended to the Departments of English, History, Government, and Psychology in the College of Liberal Arts.

The College of Engineering undertook graduate work in 1948 with six evening courses, initiated in response to the report of the Engineering Societies of New England that there was a conspicuous need, following World War II, for evening courses at the graduate level. An enrollment of 153 students in those six courses justified the addition of seven courses in the following year and in 1950 the establishment of evening Master's programs in Civil, Mechanical, and Electrical Engineering. Since that year, programs in Mathematics, Physics, Chemistry, Communications, Engineering Management, and Engineering Mechanics have been added.

The organization and development of this work has been under the direction of three men. Professor Alfred Ferretti of the Department of Mechanical Engineering was in charge for the first two years, and was followed by Professor Herbert Brown of the same department. In 1954, Professor Emil Gramstorff, Chairman of the Department of Civil Engineering, was made Dean of Graduate Engineering Programs.

The teaching personnel of the evening graduate work in engineering has been varied, including a number of men from other universities, and from research groups and industrial companies. Mr. Kentaro Tsutsumi, Principal Engineer, Jackson and Moreland, Inc., has taught courses every year since 1948.

In 1956, the Co-operative Plan was adapted to graduate study in engineering. The two-year schedule is made up of four ten-week sessions in daytime classes and the same number of weeks on industrial jobs, in teaching, or in graduate assistantships at the University. The Master's degree in Civil, Mechanical, and Electrical Engineering is made possible by this program.

The School of Business of the Evening Division started a Master of Business Administration program in 1951. As in other specialized areas, business in the post-war period needed more and more workers with advanced study and graduate degrees. Other colleges of the Greater Boston area were taking care of students available for full-time study; Northeastern undertook to serve business and industrial workers who were available only for evening study but who wanted to compete for promotion and company upgrading.

The College of Education began graduate work as well as undergraduate work in 1953. At the June Commencement of 1954, three Ed.M. degrees were conferred on students who had come to Northeastern with substantial transfer credit. Since that year, graduates of the advanced curricula have gone from Northeastern to teaching positions in all of the New England states, New York, New Jersey, Pennsylvania, California, Texas, and Oregon; others have gone on to further graduate study in education.

The Graduate School of the University, established in 1958, now administers the various programs that have developed during the past twenty years. Dr. Arthur Vernon, Chairman of the Department of Chemistry in 1938 and in 1940 Director of Graduate Study, College of Liberal Arts, is Dean of the Graduate School. He continues as Director of Graduate Programs in Arts and Sciences. Emil Gramstorff acts as Dean of Graduate Engineering Programs, and Professor Myron Spencer and Dr. Lester Vander Werf direct the graduate programs in Business Administration and Education.

(10) Paralleling the development of graduate study at Northeastern was the beginning of a process of systematizing technical research and bringing it under University sponsorship.

In the early decades, when all energies were directed to the physical development of Northeastern and the improvement and accreditation of schools and curricula, research and creative academic writing by members of the faculty were limited by heavy teaching schedules and additional assignments of committee and student advisory work. In a small way, however, research was carried out, along with the writing of textbooks and professional papers; from 1930 to 1940 some members of the faculty, particularly in the Departments of Civil and Chemical Engineering, did consulting work for industrial companies.

The first effort at formalizing research was the Bureau of Business Research, established in 1939 with Asa S. Knowles, then Dean of the College of Business Administration, as Director; other active members of the Bureau were Professors Julian Jackson, Alfred D'Alessandro, and John Tuthill. Bulletins from the Bureau, in sequence with papers from departments of the Colleges of Engineering and Liberal Arts, were issued as "Northeastern University Publications." Contributors to this series of sixteen bulletins, extending from 1940 to 1945 and the final four numbers in the years 1949 to 1951, included Professor George Pihl, Department of Electrical Engineering; Professor Chester Baker, Department of Chemical Engineering; Dr. Fay Luder and Professor Saverio Zuffanti, Department of Chemistry; and Dr. Stanley G. Estes, Department of Psychology.

Numbers 1 and 4 in the series—"Merit Rating in Industry" and "Merit Rating of Supervisors, Foremen and Department Heads" were written by Dean Knowles of the Bureau of Business Research in 1940, when merit rating in industry was coming into prominence as a subject of technical study; the bulletins were basic contributions to a new field and were widely used during the next fifteen years.

In 1954, research activities were brought under a Faculty Committee on Development and Co-ordination of Research, with Dr. William White as Chairman; and as Secretary, Dr. Ralph Troupe, who carried the new title Research Professor of Chemical Engineering. By the year 1954, research activities had become varied and were becoming extensive.

Consulting work in the Department of Chemical Engineering had led to outside financial support of projects conducted by faculty members assisted by senior students or laboratory assistants. One illustration is annual grants from Godfrey L. Cabot, Inc. for studies carried on by Professor Baker and student assistants, including Stuart Stoddard, Class of 1941, who later became a Vice President of the Cabot Company.

In 1948, the Department of Electrical Engineering received a contract for research work for the Air Force Cambridge Research Center. This initial contract led to the development of five long-range projects in succeeding years: Principles and Techniques of Speech Analysis, Research in Statistical Communications Theory and Reliability, Instrumentation for Geophysical Research, Research in Telemetering, and research directed to finding new ways of applying mathematics to engineering. Professor Martin Essigmann directed and built up the general program with Dr. Sze-Hou Chang and Professors J. Spencer Rochefort and Louis Nardone in charge of individual projects.

Under the leadership of Dr. Roger Hamilton, the College of Business Administration activated a Bureau of Business and Economic Research in 1953. Dr. William Miernyk was made Director of the Bureau, which in its first year conducted studies in "Inter-Industry Labor Mobility: The Case of the Displaced Textile Worker," "Trends and Cycles in the American Cotton Textile Industry," and "Mansfield Master-Plan." Later work of the Bureau included a Reprint Series—articles contributed by the Director and his research associates to professional journals and reviews; "Preparation and Use of Business Case Studies," developed by Professor Charles Dufton and student assistants; and "The Recruitment, Utilization and Development of Engineering Faculties," conducted by the Bureau for the committee on Development of Engineering Faculties of the American Society of Engineering Education.

In the College of Liberal Arts, the Department of Psychology carried out contracts with the U.S. Quartermaster Corps, Research and Development Command, involving studies in human variables in motor vehicle accidents and in performance of sensory and motor tasks by males of military age.

As outside contracts and grants-in-aid developed, the Faculty Committee on Development and Co-ordination of Research recommended that a Northeastern University Basic Research Fund be established. The recommendation was implemented in 1957, and three grants were made for research projects in the Departments of Biology, Sociology, and Chemical Engineering.

Concurrently, a research policy was formulated by the central Committee. On acceptance of the premise that profitable university instruction in the twentieth century requires provision for research by teachers who are competent and interested, and that a university must offer opportunities for research in order to attract and retain superior teachers, the Northeastern policy was directed toward basic, uncommitted research for the extension and transmission of knowledge, "to enhance the effectiveness of the educational program through the stimulating influence upon faculty members of sharing in the continued search for new knowledge and better understanding at the boundaries of their fields."

In 1959, another step in the development and co-ordination of research programs and projects was taken by the appointment of Dr. Carl Muckenhoupt as Director of Research. Dr. Muckenhoupt was a member of the Northeastern faculty from 1929 to 1946; for the last eleven of those years he was Chairman of the Department of Physics. After acting as Office of Naval Research Liaison Officer for Navy-sponsored research programs being carried·out in New England colleges, he came back to Northeastern to direct an area of research which had grown from spare-time efforts by individual teachers to a complex structure involving extensive personnel, facilities, and funds.

    ✻ ✻ ✻ ✻ ✻ ✻ ✻ ✻ ✻ ✻

By these ten major adaptations, during a period of thirty years, Northeastern resolved its growing pains as it moved toward maturity as a university. In summary, they represent the launching of two colleges, the closing of three schools, the elimination of responsibility for one day school and five branches of evening work, the commitment to co-education throughout the University system, and the development and encouragement of graduate work and applied research. All of these moves were efforts "to discover and to meet important needs in the field of higher education."

VII

A HOME IS BUILT

For forty years Northeastern was a growing institution without a home of its own in which it could live an independent life and plan a future. During that period it was housed in parental quarters; elsewhere, at different times, it was guest or tenant.

Until 1910 the educational work was carried on in the YMCA building on Boylston Street, but early in that year, on January 10, the building burned completely. The Directors of the Boston YMCA had earlier planned for a change of location, had decided on a site on the northwest corner of Arlington and Newbury Streets as the location for a new central building, and had established a building fund for use in the future.

Following the Boylston Street fire, the work of the YMCA, including evening classes and the few day classes, continued uninterrupted. For three months classes were held in rooms provided by the City of Boston, the Boston Young Men's Christian Union, Boston University, and M.I.T., and then in a large frame building on Ashburton Place. Two years later that building was sold to the Boston City Club, and during another interim period the educational work was carried on, according to a contemporary report, in "various buildings on Huntington and Massachusetts Avenues."

The Directors of the YMCA, in the meantime, had decided not to use the Arlington Street location but to erect a central

*Huntington Avenue Building of the Boston YMCA, built in 1913 —
photograph taken in 1943, before the building of Dodge Library in the
foreground*

building on Huntington Avenue, because of the large recreation
field to the west of the new site and because the Huntington
Avenue section of Back Bay was being rapidly developed and
was regarded as an important new center in the expansion of
Boston.

Buildings which later became landmarks were being constructed during this first decade of the century—Symphony
Hall and Horticultural Hall, 1900; the New England Conservatory of Music building, 1901; the extension of the Christian
Science Church from the original Mother Church built twelve

76

years earlier, 1906; the first of the six architectural sections of the Museum of Fine Arts, 1907; the Boston Opera House, 1908.

Huntington Avenue was the central thoroughfare into and through this growing district. In 1875 it had been laid out from Boylston Street to Camden (now Gainsborough) Street; later it was extended by sections until in 1895 it reached the Brookline town line.

The avenue was named for Ralph Huntington (1784-1866), a banker and trader important to the expansion of the Back Bay area. He was President of the Boston & Roxbury Corporation which built the famous Mill-Dam, and was involved in subsequent enterprises of water power and the development of new land in the Back Bay. Among Mr. Huntington's public interests was a concern for education; in recognition of his gifts to M.I.T. the assembly hall in the Rogers Building on Boylston Street, a handsome hall used for many public and general meetings including Lowell Lectures and the rehearsals of the Handel and Haydn Society, bore his name.

Ground breaking for the main building of the YMCA on Huntington Avenue took place in November of 1911, but a month earlier the Vocational Building, now the Botolph Building, had been completed, and was occupied by the Automobile School and Electrical School, which moved from temporary quarters on Harcourt Street. The main building was completed and occupied in 1913.

The growth of Northeastern which followed World War I necessitated space outside of the YMCA building. In 1920, classrooms and instructional offices were set up on the rented third floor of the Gainsboro Building. When the Huntington Building was completed in 1924, with a second story built "to specifications for Northeastern University," the Gainsboro Building was vacated. From 1924 until the completion of Richards Hall in 1938, Northeastern classrooms, offices, and laboratories extended, by successive areas, from Gainsborough Street to Symphony Hall—the entire second floor of the Huntington Building.

During this period, Northeastern built its own first classroom area by adding in 1936 a wing to the Botolph Building, used to meet the utilitarian needs of a maintenance shop and a print shop as well as the need for classrooms and laboratories for the new Department of Biology.

Both of the rented areas on Huntington Avenue were makeshift quarters in which education was accomplished in spite of handicaps. In the Gainsboro Building the rooms were adequate, but they were attractive to mice, rats and other noncollegiate transients from a drug store and a restaurant on the lower floors. The building contained an elevator, restricted to faculty use and inclined to break down between floors. In the Huntington Building, teachers competed with the noise of traffic, including surface streetcars, and the sounds, odors, and distracting allure of night-club restaurants and other enterprises which occupied the first floor of the building. Several classrooms, unofficially known as "squash courts," had no windows and were ventilated by skylight vents which functioned with decreasing efficiency as the years passed.

In this setting, as well as in the YMCA building and the Botolph Building, day and evening classes were conducted, a growing program of extracurricular activities was carried on, and in all respects the University not only survived but made progress. Clear evidence of that progress, and of planning for the future, is the slow, methodical effort to acquire land on which, at some future, undetermined date, Northeastern could build a home of its own.

The first purchase of land, from the Boston and Providence Railroad Corporation, took place in 1929, made possible by carefully guarded funds that had accumulated in the previous six years during which Northeastern financial accounts had been separated from those of the Boston YMCA. The land itself was not impressive—slightly more than one acre in extent, located in a wasteland area to the south of the YMCA building, about three hundred feet back from Huntington Avenue and with no legal means of access from the street to the new land

holding. It was, however, a beginning and a significant purchase; for the first time, Northeastern University owned tan-
gible, permanent property in its own name.

In the following year, 1930, three pieces of land and two
buildings were added to the small beginning. On Huntington
Avenue, the YMCA conveyed to Northeastern nearly two acres
of land lying between the street and the isolated acre purchased
in the previous year; YMCA tennis courts and a small handball
building remained on this land for some years thereafter. The
YMCA also conveyed title to the Vocational (Botolph) Building
and the land on which it stood. On Kent Street in Brookline, the
University purchased the five-acre plot which for several years
had been used as an athletic field by Northeastern and the
Huntington School, and on it built a field house.

These early properties, minor in contrast to later developments, mark the beginning of almost continuous activity over
a period of twenty-two years in accumulating the Huntington
Avenue campus. By final purchases in 1951 the central campus
on the south side of the Avenue was established as an area of
approximately twelve acres, with a street frontage of 1,300 feet.
This total result was made possible by the acquisition of fourteen separate parcels of land, one a mere scrap of 1,290 square
feet. Numerous previous owners were involved, although major
portions of the land were held by the Boston Elevated Railway
Company and The Durant, Incorporated, a private organization which had planned to build a residence hotel for working
women. Establishing lines, clearing titles, and other technical
and legal complexities necessitated hours of planning and detailed work the total of which is beyond estimate. All were part
of a systematic, progressive program of expansion and development.

Central figures in the acquisition of land and the clearing of
titles, from 1929 onward, were Dr. Ell; Dr. Churchill; Mr.
Light; and Professor Charles O. Baird, who in 1930 began
working on land surveys and the intricate details of the Land
Courting of property, and in 1954 became University Engineer.

Origin and Development of Northeastern University

The geographic section of Boston of which the Northeastern campus became a part has a long and varied history. Before the Ice Age of 20,000 years ago, a large river, possibly the Merrimac, flowed through the Back Bay area with the center of its channel cutting across the present location of Northeastern; this ancient topography accounts for the fact that bed rock under the campus is two hundred feet, more or less at different points, below the surface.

Much later, but still before recorded history, the area became useful to primitive men. When excavations for the Boylston Street subway were being made in 1913, and excavations later for the foundations of buildings, thousands of stakes distributed over an area of deeply buried mud flats and marshland were identified as the remains of a fishweir, estimated to have been in use at least 1,400 and perhaps 2,500 years ago.

Explorers and settlers of the seventeenth century found a wide expanse of tidewater marshland extending from the harbor to the hills of later-named Brookline and Roxbury; the references in 1634 to the "backside" of the Charles River appear to be the source of the designation "Back Bay."

In the nineteenth century a major extension of the terrain of Boston took place in the Back Bay. The Boston & Roxbury Mill Corporation, formed in 1814, built a wide dam from Boston Common to Sewall's Point in Brookline, and a cross dam to Roxbury. The purpose was to produce tidewater power, but the dams were also constructed as toll roads; the main dam, called both Mill-Dam and Western Avenue, followed the present line of Beacon Street and was a novel setting for buggy and cutter rides, and races between sporty drivers of high spirited horses.

The construction of railroad lines across the Back Bay, heading for Providence and Worcester, disturbed the drainage and tidal flow. In 1849 a report to the Boston City Council protested that the Back Bay was "nothing less than a great cesspool." Soon thereafter the filling of the area began, to eliminate a public nuisance and to meet a pressing need for land brought

80

about by high rents in central Boston and the building of stores on downtown streets which formerly had been residential.

From 1856 to 1894 the Back Bay took on its modern land structure. The Commonwealth filled in one hundred acres between Arlington Street and Fairfield Street, and sold house lots at public auction; it also donated new land on Boylston Street to M.I.T. and to the Museum of Natural History. An enterprising company built a railroad line to Needham and by using trains of thirty-five cars to haul fill, produced two building lots a day, on "good" days.

Streets were laid out on the new land but were changed and renamed as the district grew and was modified by the demands of new decades. Forsyth Street, for example, was successively named Bryant Street, Bryant Mall, and Rogers Avenue; and sections of it were designated as Ruggles Place and Silver Lane. Hemenway Street originally ran from Boylston Street to Huntington Avenue and until 1898 was known as Parker Street. Attached to the street names of the area are many interesting and curious associations, but none more so than those of Botolph Street. According to the traditional story of England, Saint Botolph founded a monastery, in the seventh century, in a then ancient town known as Ikanho. Later, out of reverence for Saint Botolph, the town changed its name to Botolphstown, and still later contracted the name to Boston.

By the beginning of the twentieth century the Back Bay was established as an important section of Boston, but it still was spotted with large open areas. The field on Huntington Avenue which had appealed to the Directors of the Boston YMCA when they bought land for their new building was the scene of varied and famous activities. Here, in 1903, was played the first World Series baseball game, between the Boston Americans and the Pittsburgh Nationals, with the home team the winner. In later years the Ringling Brothers and Barnum and Bailey Circus raised its tents in the open field, and the Tabernacle of the evangelist Billy Sunday was there in 1916. Another stimulating occupant was the Shoot the Chute, in which adventure-

*First World Series baseball game, 1903 — the Cabot Physical Education
Center now occupies this area*

some citizens slid in toboggan cars down a long incline and
into a pool of water. After other and incidental uses, and many
transfers of ownership, these acres on Huntington Avenue,
facing the Fenway, became the Northeastern campus.

A memorandum on "Plant Development Plan for Northeastern University," prepared by Dr. Churchill in 1948, reports that
on June 14, 1933, Mr. Dodge as Chairman of the Board of
Trustees appointed a Committee on Housing, comprised of
seven men with Mr. Dodge and Dr. Speare as ex-officio mem-

bers. Early in 1934 this committee presented a plan for securing a design for the development of a University plant and the plan was accepted by the Board. An architectural competition was held and on June 11, 1934, the Jury of Award, made up of the Committee on Housing and the Executive Council of the University, having examined the five plans which had been submitted, approved the one prepared by Coolidge, Shepley, Bulfinch and Abbott. In October of 1934 the Board of Trustees established a Committee on Development, for the purpose of raising funds for the construction of the first building in the development plan.

An objective backward view to the years 1933 and 1934 would suggest that these decisions and plans were ill timed and so visionary as to be impossibly unrealistic.

The stock market crash of 1929, with an estimated loss to American citizens of forty billion dollars, had initiated a period of business depression and of national insecurity, both economic and psychological. Suicides of business executives, apple selling in the streets of great cities, the collapse of over four thousand state and national banks during the period 1930 to 1932, dust bowl farmers facing with shotguns the agents of foreclosure, the march to Washington of armed forces veterans —all these were harrowing experiences. In 1933 they were still grim realities.

The year 1933 was marked by the first recorded sit-down strike, the Senate investigation of Wall Street (immortalized by the midget on the knee of J. P. Morgan), the nagging problem of unemployment, and other disturbing evidences of national insecurity and maladjustment. While the vigorous activities of the Roosevelt administration gave reassurance to some Americans, to others it increased the common temper of skepticism and alarm. Such slight signs of confidence as the revival of the Miss America beauty contest after a lapse of five years were lost in an atmosphere of confusion and defeatism.

The spectre of the times—a new enemy in the history of the United States—was undefined but universal fear. In the last months of his Presidency, Herbert Hoover said in precise terms, "Ninety per cent of our difficulty in depressions is caused by fear." Franklin Roosevelt at his inauguration on March 4, 1933, said, in words that stirred emotion and imagination, "The only thing we have to fear is fear itself—nameless, unreasoning, unjustified terror which paralyzes needed efforts to convert retreat into advance."

The optimism and self-confidence of the men who controlled the destiny of Northeastern is demonstrated by the fact that in this critical period of national demoralization they adopted a plan of development which called for six buildings at an estimated cost of $3,688,000. Moreover, from 1933 to 1937, while the country struggled upward from the lowest points of depression and despair, these men built the first building of the plan and financed in advance most of its cost.

The public announcement in 1934 of the architectural plan was, to be sure, cautious: "The University is not prepared to announce just when construction will be started, inasmuch as a campaign for funds is required before the buildings are constructed." The same press release, however, also said, "The University has reason to feel that in the not-far-distant future the first two buildings will be built."

The need for the first building of the adopted plan had become critical as insurance of the future of the College of Engineering. From 1936 to 1938 the new Engineers' Council for Professional Development conducted an accrediting program designed to control professional standards in the training of engineers, as had been done earlier in the training of aspirants to the practice of law and medicine. At Northeastern it became apparent, after one examination by ECPD, that the College of Engineering could not meet the requirements of the accrediting body until it was provided with adequate classrooms, laboratories, and other facilities. Since the future of Northeastern depended at that time on the future of its College of Engineering, the construction of a building was imperative.

A Home is Built

Fortunately, the leaders of the University had the will and determination to undertake expansion in a period which even then was regarded as inauspicious if not ominous.

Funds for the first building were raised by a widespread solicitation which included faculty, staff, students, alumni, members of the newly formed Corporation, and friends of the University. In most instances the contributions were individually small and extended over a three-year period, but when the building was completed, its $800,000 cost had been met except for a mortgage which was cleared in 1940, the first year of Dr. Ell's presidency.

Ground was broken for the building on September 29, 1937; the cornerstone was laid in November. These two ceremonies, and the later dedication of the building, were the last major occasions at which Dr. Speare officiated before his retirement as President.

When the new structure was occupied in June of 1938 it was designated as West Building, while the educational area of the YMCA was called East Building, and, to complete the compass designations, the Botolph Building became the South Building.

On October 3, 1938, Northeastern held "Fortieth Anniversary and Dedicatory Exercises" in the Boston Opera House. The new building was dedicated, as was also the School of Law Building at 47 Mt. Vernon Street, earlier purchased and renovated to prepare, in part, for day classes in law which began in September of that year.

An address was delivered by Karl T. Compton, then President of the Massachusetts Institute of Technology, and Dr. Speare conferred honorary degrees upon Mr. Compton; Winthrop W. Aldrich, Chairman of the Board of Directors of the Chase National Bank; Harvey N. Davis, President of the Stevens Institute of Technology; Dugald C. Jackson, Professor Emeritus and Honorary Lecturer at the Massachusetts Institute of Technology; Henry Cabot Lodge, Jr., United States Senator

Richards Hall, completed in 1938 — first unit of the Northeastern building plan

from Massachusetts; and Edward A. Weeks, Jr., Editor of the *Atlantic Monthly.*

The West Building made possible new and adequate classrooms, laboratories, administrative offices, an enlarged Bookstore, and general service areas. Particularly important were the new quarters of the Department of Chemistry, dedicated at the October exercises as the Charles Hayden Memorial Laboratories. Remaining in the educational section of the YMCA building were classrooms, several instructional offices, and the library.

Two years later the Board of Trustees voted to give the new building a permanent name, and on May 7, 1941, as a part of Corporation Day, a tablet in the first-floor lobby was unveiled.

A Home is Built

The inscription is:

RICHARDS HALL

NAMED FOR

JAMES LORIN RICHARDS

INDUSTRIALIST AND PHILANTHROPIST

HIS VISION, ENERGY, AND

DEVOTION TO THE NEEDS OF YOUTH

MADE THIS BUILDING POSSIBLE

Mr. Richards had become a valuable and substantial friend of Northeastern. In 1932, the second year in which the University conferred honorary degrees, he was awarded the honorary degree of Doctor of Laws, with the citation: "Organizer, industrialist and financier, who, as a self-made man, by dint of superior ability, tact, energy, and vision, steadily advanced to outstanding achievements in business, becoming a leader in the gas and transportation industries and in many other types of business enterprises; one who, because of his great attainments and his human sympathy, kindliness, and integrity serves as an inspiration to youth and is held in high esteem by his associates and the general business world."

In 1935, Mr. Richards became a member of the Board of Trustees, and in the next year a charter member of the new University Corporation; he was also helpful in the formation of the Corporation by enlisting members from his wide circle of business and civic associates.

During Northeastern's first effort at fund raising, Mr. Richards was responsible for securing more than half of the cost of the building which now perpetuates his name and his contribution to the establishment of Northeastern.

Mr. Richards died in 1955, less than a week before he would have reached his ninety-seventh birthday. For nearly seventy years of that life span, he was a dominant figure in the industrial development and modernization of eastern Massachusetts, but with interests and influence extending beyond New England. In the last years of his life his biography was written by

William T. Cloney, Jr., then a member of the Department of English.

In September of 1940, Dr. Ell, in his third month as President of the University, reported to the Board of Trustees that the West Building and the other available areas could not long contain the expanding programs of Northeastern. He also reported that he had accumulated $30,000 in gifts for a building fund to be used in the future, and he then proposed that in view of worsening world conditions a smaller structure than the West Building should be undertaken immediately at a cost of $250,000, and asked for authorization to raise the necessary funds.

The result was a building constructed during the tightening war year of 1941, when materials and costs presented an increasing problem of planning and execution. The "New Building" provided space for the Department of Chemical Engineering, an enlarged Department of Biology, a temporary student lunch room, instructional offices, and classrooms, including a large lecture hall. The "New Building" was later named "Science Hall."

The third building was initiated when the Corporation voted, in April, 1944, to raise $1,000,000 for further construction. The proposal was a generalized one, since the intention was to add at some time in the future a building primarily for use by students in recreational and extracurricular activities, with an auditorium and a gymnasium to be added at an even later date.

By 1944 the original plant design had been revised conspicuously. The connection of all of the planned buildings had been discarded in favor of separate buildings with a connecting basement passage, since it became apparent that above-ground fusion of the buildings would result in wide and useless corridors and a reduction of lighting from outside. The central building had been designated as a "Student Activities Building" and "Gymnasium and Auditorium," but a detailed study of property lines and possible land areas proved that a gymnasium and auditorium could not be combined.

A *Home is Built*

During the planning and construction of the Student Center, Dr. Ell again exercised his initiative, not only in raising funds but in making sure that the building would be complete and permanent. Although the auditorium had been planned as a later addition, Dr. Ell, with typical forthright decisiveness, authorized the ordering of steel for the entire building, and thereby insured the construction of the auditorium.

Alumni Auditorium is a testimony to the response by alumni to a campaign conducted from 1945 to 1947. Hundreds of chairs in the body of the auditorium bear the names of contributing graduates. In the lobby is a plaque listing those alumni who made special contributions.

The Student Center Building and Alumni Auditorium were dedicated on October 5, 1947. Thomas C. Clark, then Attorney General of the United States, was the principal guest and speaker. Among the greetings was that of Robert Bruce, '14, Chairman of the Alumni Federation, who said,

"I cannot conceive of any alumnus coming into this impressive auditorium, named for the alumni, without experiencing a thrill of pride and satisfaction in his relationship to Northeastern and a sense of having a vested interest and an obligation to advance, in whatever manner he may be able, the best interests of this great institution."

In the years since 1947, Alumni Auditorium has been the scene of many events important in the history of Northeastern. Two from the University's "Fiftieth Anniversary Year" are especially significant.

On June 18, 1948, a Gold Star Memorial Service was held, participated in by Dr. Ell, Dean Harold Melvin, Dean Charles Havice, Professor Robert Bruce, the Rev. Wilbur Ziegler '40, and the Rev. Oliver Childers '38. The service was a tribute to the 5520 Northeastern men who served in World War II, and a plaque in the lobby of the auditorium carries 241 names under the inscription "In grateful memory of Northeastern Men who gave their lives for their country 1941–1945."

The Fiftieth Anniversary Convocation was held in Alumni

Auditorium on October 2, 1948. James Bryant Conant, then President of Harvard University, gave an address in which he stated his view of education which in later years he developed more fully:

"The increasing emphasis on diversity and flexibility is closely related to our American ideas of what constitutes a democracy . . . in this country we have evolved a type of fluid and free society never seen in the world before.

"We plan for education of all youth, not a selected few . . . we aim at social equality of all useful labor and refuse to have our post-high school education a narrow channel leading only to learned professions."

Honorary degrees were conferred at the Fiftieth Anniversary Convocation, and two were particularly impressive.

The Board of Trustees, in secret session, had voted to award an honorary Doctor of Laws degree to Robert Gray Dodge, their Chairman, in recognition of "a most unusual service to the University."

Dr. Ell announced that the Board of Trustees had voted to confer the honorary degree of Doctor of Literature on Rabbi Joshua Liebman, before his death in June of 1948. Dr. Ell said: "Rabbi Liebman is not here to receive the degree, but his spirit is still alive in the community. The memory of his greatness of mind and heart remains to guide and encourage us. In his own enduring words: 'Life will not perish with us; humanity will not die. Culture will not disappear with our generation . . . live for the triumph of men whom we shall never know, of ages we shall never experience.'"

At the dinner in honor of Dr. Ell on October 22, 1958, the Chairman of the Corporation, Robert Dodge, announced that the Student Center Building had been renamed the Carl Stephens Ell Student Center. The formal designation of the building by that name took place as a part of Alumni Day on June 19, 1959.

Northeastern's library was for many years one of the critical points of growth and development. Originally it consisted of additions to the library which the Boston YMCA provided for its members; by 1929 it was a separate collection consisting of 12,740 books. Miss Myra White, associated with Northeastern from 1920 until her retirement in 1957, built the library resources from small beginnings to a pattern of materials and organization needed for a university.

The addition of a library building to Northeastern's campus was determined in time by three factors: the overflow in quantity of the library itself, the need by the YMCA for the space occupied by the Northeastern library, and the national and international complications leading to the Korean conflict of 1950.

These conditions accelerated the program of planning, fund raising, and building. In August, 1950, the Board of Trustees voted to proceed with immediate construction, six months ahead of planned schedule, and ground was broken on August 29. The cost of construction was met by another vigorous and widespread appeal to Corporation, alumni, faculty and staff, students, and friends of the University; the success of the campaign was determined by the efforts of many people but particularly by the central committee headed by Richard L. Bowditch and Robert Cutler.

The library building, planned to house eventually 300,000 books, was in use in the summer of 1952, with the fourth floor given over to the Drawing Department and with classrooms and instructional offices occupying areas which later would be used by the library. In 1953, Roland H. Moody came to Northeastern from the Lamont Library at Harvard University as Director of the University Library, and in the following seven years built the library from 37,000 volumes to 95,000.

At the meeting of the University Corporation in May, 1959, the library was named the Robert Gray Dodge Library, in honor of the man who was teacher of the first class in law in 1898, member of the Board of Trustees in 1922, and Chairman of the Board from 1932 to 1959.

Following immediately the erection of the library building,

the construction of the Physical Education Center was begun in the summer of 1952 and completed in 1954. Funds for the building were augmented by gifts from trusts and corporations, and the Alumni Fund was used for interior equipment.

This addition to the Northeastern plant contains two gymnasiums, special exercise rooms, an indoor rifle range, offices and service areas, and, as a major unit, a cage used for work in physical education, track practice and indoor meets, and football and baseball practice. All areas and facilities of the Center are used for three phases of Northeastern work: the physical education program, the development of athletic squads, and some parts of the activity of the ROTC.

On February 26, 1957, the two related physical education buildings were named the Godfrey Lowell Cabot Physical Education Center, on the occasion of Mr. Cabot's ninety-sixth birthday.

Mr. Cabot became a member of the University Corporation in 1941 and thereafter was a valuable and influential friend of Northeastern. He first entered the records of Northeastern during the brief period at the end of World War I when the School of Co-operative Engineering was activated by the government as an SATC and Navy unit; a report of that period states: "Lt. Godfrey Cabot, USN, was helpful in securing materials and instructors."

To provide adequate quarters for the work of the Evening Division and classrooms and laboratories for the growing student population, a seventh building was raised during 1955 and 1956. Until its dedication on October 24, 1956, it was known as the "Classroom-Laboratory Building"; then it was named Hayden Hall, "in recognition of the gift from the Charles Hayden Foundation."

An interesting feature of the fund-raising for Hayden Hall was the series of special events and projects carried out by fraternities, clubs, the Silver Masque, and other student groups as contributions to the cost of construction.

When completed, Hayden Hall was occupied by the Eve-

Cabot Court

ning Division, the Department of Electrical Engineering, the College of Business Administration, and extensive instructional areas.

In July of 1958, ground was broken for the building which was to become the Graduate Center, designed to centralize the graduate work of the University and to include the Department of Physics (moved from Richards Hall) and a University cafeteria. This building was dedicated on September 8, 1959, the day of the inauguration of the third President of the University.

During the twenty-year period from 1938 to 1958, Northeastern brought to reality the campus plan which had been announced in 1934. The original plan underwent changes, but the final result was a compact set of major new buildings, constructed at a cost of $8,288,333 in two decades marked historically by national industrial depression, two periods of armed conflict, and fundamental changes in the pattern of higher education which brought strain and, in some instances, confusion to American colleges and universities.

During the same period, Northeastern extended its property and facilities beyond the central campus. Four additions were adjacent to the Huntington Avenue plant.

In 1947 and 1948, land bounded by Hemenway, St. Stephen, and Forsyth Streets was acquired. This plot of nearly four acres was, like other Back Bay land, an area which had passed through many hands since its reclamation from tidewater marshes; five owners were involved in the negotiations which resulted in final purchase. The land became the North Parking Area, and included tennis courts, and, until the building of the Physical Education Center, limited space for track practice. The limitation of the space was dramatized when during one track practice session a zealous participant in the field events hurled the hammer over the Northeastern boundaries and to the top of a parked car which, perhaps fortunately, was owned by a member of the Northeastern faculty.

The Tufts Medical and Dental Buildings on Huntington Avenue were purchased by Northeastern in 1949, when Tufts University moved its schools to an in-town location. After razing two of the three buildings, Northeastern occupied the Greenleaf Building, establishing there headquarters for the ROTC, and new quarters for the Department of Industrial Engineering and for electronics research laboratories.

In 1951, a building on Forsyth Street, vacated by the Sylvania Electric Products Company and at an earlier stage in its history a garage, was added to the Northeastern property. It was remodeled to become the Forsyth Building, to provide additional areas for the ROTC and instructional departments.

By the mid-1950's, the Boston Opera House had become a

University Yard

liability to its owners, and in 1956 it was condemned as unsafe by the City of Boston. Northeastern bought the land and building, later removed the building, and used the land as a parking area, but with the intention of constructing in the future a building on the land facing Huntington Avenue and the main campus, and adjoining the North Parking Area.

The increase in student enrollment in the Day Colleges from beyond commuting distance led to the first Northeastern dormitory in 1950, a remodeled residence on Marlboro Street which was occupied in that year by twenty-two women students. In later years, four additional dormitories were established in the Back Bay for both women and men students.

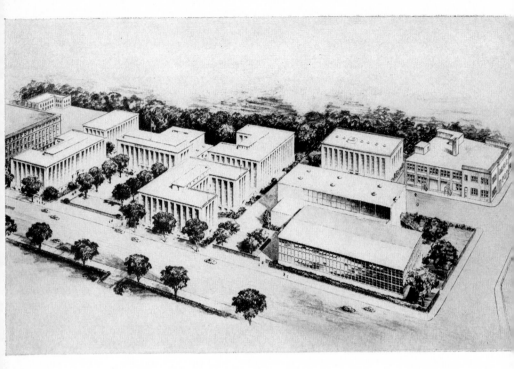

Central Campus, Huntington Avenue

By 1960 Northeastern could well say that it had a home of its own. That home had been built painfully but carefully from the single acre of land of 1929. It was built into a permanent city campus on Huntington Avenue, with extensions and additions which laid the basis for further development and expansion in future decades.

A broad view of the building of the physical Northeastern University shows that two unusual elements explain the past and forecast the future.

The plan of development adopted in 1933 has proved to be workable and successful. Through the decades the plan was kept flexible and was subject to change and modification. Nevertheless, the present outcome is remarkably close to the estimate of 1933 in actual buildings and in meeting the Northeastern needs which at that time could only be conjectured.

96

A Home is Built

Through the combination of chance and foresight, Northeastern is located in a section of Boston which in the future will become increasingly significant as a specialized community.

In the early years of the present century the Back Bay was a new, open area, in contrast to the other outlying sides of Boston where established residential streets, industrial interests, and the waterfront precluded extensive expansion. Inevitably, schools, hospitals, art centers, social service homes, and other institutions gravitated to the Back Bay; among those institutions was the Boston YMCA. Since land was available and inexpensive, each institution secured all the space it needed then or believed it could need in the foreseeable future.

The future, however, brought development and expansion which could not possibly have been foreseen. By mid-century, the established permanent institutions in the Back Bay were cramped for space, and were facing common problems of the need for additional land, and needs for improved commuting transportation, parking areas, and housing for permanent and temporary residence of employees and patrons. Many institutions had become established occupants, notably the New England Conservatory of Music, the Museum of Fine Arts, the Harvard Medical School, the hospitals and medical centers of the Longwood Avenue area, Simmons College, Emmanuel College, and the Gardner Museum. At the same time, the Back Bay had proved to be a variable institutional area; new members came in, while such early institutions as Tufts Medical School, the Boston Opera House, and Mechanics Hall disappeared from the scene.

Northeastern is therefore centrally located in an active, growing segment of Boston. The nature and function of the Back Bay has been determined by its history; its potential is undetermined and unlimited. In the future, Northeastern will of necessity work to meet its own needs and will share the common interests of other institutions in the further development and the long-range stabilization of the Back Bay as a community of educational, cultural, and social service residents.

97

VIII

FIFTY YEARS OF CO-OPERATIVE
EDUCATION

During the first half of the twentieth century, the co-operative plan of education grew from experimental beginnings to the status of a permanent and significant form of higher education. Northeastern University, the second educational institution to adopt the co-operative plan, established and has maintained a central position in the historical development of this method of academic-industrial training.

Modern co-operative education originated in the pioneer efforts of Herman Schneider, who adapted to his time the principle of co-ordinating theory and the application of theory which had been thought and written about and in a small way practiced for several centuries.

After his early years in a Pennsylvania mining town, Mr. Schneider was graduated from Lehigh University in 1894 as an architect. Varied experiences in architecture, in railroad construction in the Northwest, and as an instructor in civil engineering at Lehigh University led to a serious analytical consideration of the proper training for engineers. Mr. Schneider saw engineering curricula of that time as merely an extension of traditional liberal arts education, conducted in an isolated academic setting. He believed that for technical students the classroom and the outside world could be related, and that the young engineer should learn methods, processes, and practices during his college years rather than afterward. He also foresaw

98

possibilities of adapting his thinking to commercial, business, and liberal arts undergraduate education.

Having formulated a plan which to him seemed theoretically sound and at the same time workable, Mr. Schneider met with resistance and opposition ranging from skepticism to scorn. Educators and business men found the proposal interesting but in their opinion completely impractical. High school graduates were reluctant to undertake a program of six years, leading to a degree which they could earn in four years of conventional education. Mr. Schneider spent five years in a continuous effort to win support and the opportunity to put his plan into action.

In 1906 at the University of Cincinnati, where Mr. Schneider had been a member of the faculty for three years, an experimental year of co-operative engineering education was undertaken, involving fifteen Cincinnati companies who employed six pairs each of mechanical and electrical engineering students, and three students of chemical engineering, one without an alternate. This group started a six-year program of work and study in alternating units of one week. At the end of the first year, Mr. Schneider was authorized to continue the program, and co-operative education was under way.

As Dean and later President of the University of Cincinnati, Herman Schneider saw his experiment firmly established, not only at his university but elsewhere. By the year of his death, 1939, his plan had been adopted by forty American colleges and universities. Some institutions dropped it after a trial period, others made minor or drastic changes in the original concept and its application, but the co-operative plan had become an accepted and respected addition to the pattern of American higher education.

In Boston, co-operative education was initiated in 1909 with "Co-Operative Engineering Courses" conducted by the day Polytechnic School of the YMCA Evening Institute. Eight young men started four years of courses on one-week alternating periods of classroom study and employment in Boston industrial companies. In the following year the Institute announced curricula in Civil and Mechanical Engineering and in Chemistry; in 1911–1912 Electrical Engineering was added and Chemistry was changed to Chemical Engineering. The 1912–1913 catalog was issued under the name "Co-Operative Engineering School."

These programs did not lead to an academic degree, but the appeal and value of co-operative education in the Boston area is shown by statistical evidence. By 1913–1914, for example, the original enrollment of eight had increased to 107, and the four co-operating companies had increased to fourteen. In the following years, and in spite of World War I, the figures grew steadily.

In 1920 Northeastern College was authorized to grant degrees in its Co-operative School of Engineering, and in 1936 the school became the present College of Engineering, including the four original curricula and Industrial Engineering, which developed from a curriculum in Administrative Engineering, added in 1921.

Northeastern built its day colleges on the premise of the co-operative plan of education. Full-time study was made available during several brief periods through the decades, primarily in times of educational stress caused by economic and world conditions, but as the Colleges of Business Administration, Liberal Arts, and Education were added to the structure of the University, they were developed in an educational plan parallel to that of the College of Engineering.

The progress and status of the co-operative plan at Northeastern have been directed, both in principle and precept and in the mechanics of operation, by five men in succession.

Hercules W. Geromanos, as Dean of the Polytechnic School, administered the plan in its first years. With help from Frank Palmer Speare and others he introduced the new idea to Boston companies and secured commitments to accept working students in 1909; thereafter he supervised the students in their relationships with the school and with their employers.

In 1917 Carl S. Ell succeeded Mr. Geromanos as Dean, and

assumed, along with his other responsibilities, that of placing students on jobs and coordinating their study and work, as he had had a hand in doing for several previous years. During the next two-year period Dean Ell extended the roster of co-operating companies from twenty-seven to forty-two as the student body increased from 160 to 235. At that point the growth of the school made necessary a division of labor.

Philip C. Nash joined the staff of Northeastern College in 1919 as Professor of Civil Engineering and was later made Director of Engineering Practice. Mr. Nash had previously been a practicing engineer with the Boston Transit Commission and had worked on the design and construction of the South Boston Tunnel; he also had served in the United States Army in World War I as a Captain.

In February of 1921 the student newspaper *The Tech* reported that Professor Nash had been granted a leave of absence to go to Yellow Springs, Ohio, where Arthur Morgan, as President of Antioch College, was in process of reorganizing the college on a co-operative plan designed "to train proprietors and owners rather than employees." Mr. Nash established the co-operative plan at Antioch College and stayed on to become Dean of the college. Later, he was Executive Director of the League of Nations Association, and in 1933 President of the University of Toledo. In 1938, nine years before his death, Mr. Nash was the recipient of an honorary LL.D. degree from Northeastern University.

The fourth man to guide co-operative work at Northeastern, and the second to hold the title of Director of Engineering Practice, was Winthrop E. Nightingale, who in the spring of 1921 was appointed to that position and also made Assistant Professor of Civil Engineering. With the later titles of Director of Co-operative Work and Director of the Department of Co-operative Work, Winthrop Nightingale built the program through the years until his death in 1953.

The increasing size and complexity of Northeastern's co-operative education during this period of thirty-two years is indicated by growth in numbers from 433 engineering students in 1921 to the 1953 total of 2379 students in the three colleges of Engineering, Business Administration, and Liberal Arts. In the second year of his work, Professor Nightingale's staff consisted of an Assistant Director of Engineering Practice, who was also a member of the teaching faculty; at the end of his period of direction his department was made up of ten Co-ordinators of Co-operative Work.

This expansion was dominated by Professor Nightingale's systematic administrative abilities and his intense and unswerving belief in the educational values and personal disciplines of co-operative education. The 1953 senior annual, *The Cauldron*, included in its In Memoriam statement: ". . . Completely devoted to his work at the University, Professor Nightingale was highly regarded by his colleagues, by students, and by co-operating employers as a man of stalwart integrity, indefatigable energy, and splendid personal qualities."

Roy L. Wooldridge became Director of the Department of Co-operative Work in 1953 and has held the position since that time, extending and adapting the work of the department and its personnel to the changing conditions of recent years. Professor Wooldridge was graduated from Northeastern in 1945 and after four years in engineering work returned to his university as a Co-ordinator in the department which he now heads.

In the years that followed Herman Schneider's valiant experiment in Ohio, the term "co-operative education" came to be widely used. It was applied to substantial technical curricula leading to recognized academic degrees, and it was also the name given to educational experiments which in some instances were little more than extended field trips of industrial observation and some actual work. All of these uses and adaptations of the co-operative idea had values and validity. Northeastern University has been unusual in its continuous and complete use of the idea.

The completeness of use is indicated by some of the policies and practices which Northeastern established early in its development and has held to consistently.

Except during brief interludes, the colleges of the Day Division have been operated entirely on the co-operative plan. The acceptance of a student for the freshman year implies the responsibility of the University to place him on co-operative work, provided he satisfactorily completes the freshman year. Co-operative work is not optional for the student, nor is it assigned to a limited group of selected students. The University holds complete control of placement, rather than allowing students to find their own work.

Because co-operative work has been an integral part of the functioning of Northeastern, the Department of Co-operative Work has always had a voice in university administration and policy, through representation of the department on central committees of the University.

As developed by Winthrop Nightingale, a stringent policy has been the maintenance of close contact between Northeastern and co-operating companies. By systematic planning of time, co-ordinators make visits once during every ten-week period to firms within day commuting distance of the University, twice a year to outlying companies, and once a year to the most distant companies, in such states as Michigan and North Carolina. These visits accomplish several purposes; foremost is the opportunity to meet with supervisors to review the student's progress on the job and to assist the employer in improving or adapting the program to best meet his own expectations while enhancing the student's learning opportunities. These personal contacts in the field improve the co-ordinator's knowledge of his students, keep him abreast of the latest developments in his area of specialty, and perform an important public relations function for the University. On local visits the co-ordinator often does not see the student worker; at distant points, where the student is away from his home, the co-ordinator always sees him to bring him news and a reminder of his University.

A Business Conference, sponsored in 1948 by the Department of Co-operative Work, became later the Co-operating Employers' Dinner. At this annual event employers and supervisors, whom Dr. Ell often addressed in past years as "the faculty in the field," visit Northeastern and become better acquainted with the academic setting of the students whom they employ.

A deliberate effort has been made to build up diversity of employment, to avoid concentration of student workers in one industry or in a group of related industries, and thus to provide breadth of training opportunities as well as to avoid problems of readjustment should the need for students decrease in any one industry.

The Northeastern Co-operative Plan has been adjusted to changing times and conditions. Perhaps the best illustration of flexibility is the increase in the length of alternating periods of study and work.

Employers naturally prefer to have students on their jobs as long as possible, to avoid breaks in continuity and the readjustment of individuals. Likewise, teachers, especially those with traditional background, believe that students learn best and most during solid blocks of time on the campus. Dr. Ell, who played a vital part in the development of co-operative education at Northeastern, became convinced that the period of class work should equip the student with a unit of subject matter to apply on the job, but that the working period should not be of such length as to break the student's feeling of identity with his university. After experimentation with one-week, two-week, and five-week periods of alternation, the ten-week plan was adopted as the time unit providing the greatest benefits and avoiding the major disadvantages.

By the application of these policies the Co-operative Plan at Northeastern continued in operation and progressed in effectiveness, in spite of handicaps.

During the depression period of 1930 to 1935 student employment dropped sharply; Winthrop Nightingale, writing for

Industry Magazine, reported: ". . . the lowest point to which the co-operative employment curve sank was 42% of the students enrolled." Companies which wanted to retain students on their payrolls were reluctant to do so while family men were in need of work. Many helpful employers resorted to the stop-gap measure, beneficial to themselves and to students, of using students for temporary jobs as special needs arose. Many of these jobs had no relation to the students' curricula, but they provided work for compensation in a period when money was scarce. Throughout this difficult period the members of the Department of Co-operative Work continued to visit companies, both employers and prospective employers, and thereby maintained a continuity of relationship. The Northeastern Co-operative Plan was kept in the consciousness of business and industry, and groundwork was laid for future development in the post-depression years.

Even in times of prosperity the correlation of study and work has been difficult to implement in all academic curricula. Herman Schneider worked with technological students, though he thought also of students of business and the humanities. Northeastern adapted the plan to all of its colleges. Inevitably, some students saw no correlation between the jobs to which they were assigned and the subject in which they were majoring; most of them eventually recognized the basic and peripheral values of practical experience under working conditions during formative undergraduate years.

By its very nature, the co-operative plan depends for success upon complex and delicate relationships involving student, employer, co-ordinator, and at some points teacher and university administrator. These relationships can become strained and on occasion they can break down. The reason may be the unco-operative and dissatisfied student, the busy or unsympathetic employer, or the co-ordinator who has misjudged just one of the many elements in a situation which needs adjustment.

Inherent in the co-operative plan, also, are numerous subtle and intangible problems. In some companies non-college supervisors and other workers resent the visiting collegians; as a result, the student is handicapped by his academic status and if he makes a mistake, is more directly and severely criticized than he would be if he were not a student. Women students on co-operative work are less impressed by preparation for a career through experience in routine work than by an interesting job at a satisfactory wage. Some companies try the co-operative plan with little understanding of its purpose and function, and soon find reasons for abandoning it. These problems in human relations are part of the work of the co-ordinators, and part of the education of the students.

In spite of the strains imposed upon co-operative education by varying industrial conditions and the demands made on all those concerned in operating the plan, the values of co-operative education are by now well established.

Work assignments give the student a chance to see his profession in action; at graduation he is oriented to it. On the other hand, he may have decided along the way that the profession is not congenial to him, and he has been able to change his direction while still an undergraduate. The "Co-op" student learns work habits and requirements, standards and values, and the basic rules of harmonious association with other workers, and thereby accumulates during his college years the larger orientation necessary to any worker in any profession.

Since World War II, changes in attitude toward co-operative work have become apparent and have affected the operation of the plan at Northeastern as elsewhere.

The rapid expansion in many areas of business and industry has been accompanied by an increasing need for manpower trained both in general disciplines and in specialized skills and techniques. The result has been a wider acceptance of student workers and an increase in company training programs for students; in 1958–1959, for example, fifty per cent of all Northeastern co-operative work students were in planned company training programs of varying lengths and degrees of formality.

Co-ordinators find now a ready acceptance of students as

desirable employees. The students, often given opportunities to prove their ingenuity and creativity as well as their ability to do routine work, in many instances have made real contributions to their company and have been rewarded with assignments of increasing importance and responsibility. Frequently the exceptional student moves naturally into exceptional work: auditing rather than doing simple accounting, working on the development of the gas turbine engine rather than performing routine mechanical chores, writing copy for a newspaper rather than acting as a City Room errand boy.

These changes are part of a growing inter-relationship of education and the world of business, a basic shift in understanding and effort toward mutual accomplishment reflected at other points in the pattern of contemporary higher education.

The increasing importance of graduate work for engineers led to the establishment in 1956 of a co-operative program leading to the master's degree in Electrical Engineering. A year later additional programs in Mechanical and Civil Engineering were added.

After a half century of operation Northeastern continues to be a university built on and committed to co-operative education; without this plan, now tried and proved, Northeastern would not have served a valid purpose in the Boston educational community and, indeed, might not have come into being.

IX

SIXTY YEARS OF EVENING
EDUCATION

Since 1898, evening education at Northeastern has passed through successive stages of evolutionary development. In its general aspects the development has been part of the changing national pattern of evening education; at some points, innovations and variations in method and emphasis have been peculiar to Northeastern.

In the years of the YMCA Evening Institute and later under the direction of the University, evening programs were concentrated in four areas: law, college preparatory work, engineering and related technical study, and business.

The School of Law was throughout its fifty-eight years of operation an evening school, supplemented during the last years of that period by a day program.

From the establishment of the Evening Preparatory School in 1904 until the termination in 1956 of the last of the precollege courses offered by the Lincoln Preparatory School, secondary education was a small but stable and valuable part of the evening work.

The Polytechnic School of 1904 was designed to meet the needs of men and boys working in the expanding and increasingly complex technical trades of a new century. After ten years of operation the school was offering three, four, and five-year programs in Chemistry and in Chemical, Electrical, Structural, Railroad, and Municipal Engineering. The student enrolled for three courses each year. The scanty records indicate that most of the students did not complete full programs, but they undoubtedly accumulated knowledge and skills useful to them in their work.

The Polytechnic School was extremely flexible. It changed its offerings frequently, and was directed by several successive Deans, including Carl S. Ell, who was in charge of the school from 1919 to 1924. Three years later, the name Lincoln Institute was adopted, with James W. Lees as Director. Mr. Lees continued as head of the school until 1945.

In a somewhat parallel way the School of Commerce and Finance, started in 1907, developed and changed as education for business changed. Unlike the Polytechnic School, it established degree programs, in Business Administration and Professional Accounting. The Bachelor of Commercial Science degree was granted to a student who was a high school graduate, who passed the four-year sequence of courses with at least a grade of C, and who had had two years of "satisfactory business experience." The requirements for the Master of Commercial Science degree were the bachelor's degree, a year of study "under the direction of the faculty," and a general examination at the end of the year.

Comparative figures show that the School of Commerce and Finance enrolled more students than did the Polytechnic School, especially in the years following World War I when Northeastern was conducting programs in outlying cities. The direction of the school was carried out by eleven different men from 1907 to 1945; of this group, Carl D. Smith served longest as Dean, from 1923 to 1935. During his administration, in 1928, the school became the School of Business.

As the decades of the present century passed, conspicuous changes in concepts and premises as well as in content and method took place at most American colleges and universities which conducted evening education. These changes are reflected by the contrast in the names which colleges formerly used and now use to designate their evening programs. The early terms, so consistently used as to be almost universal, were "night school" and "adult education." Both terms came to have circumscribed and, in many quarters, slightly negative connotations. A night school was assumed, especially by educational traditionalists, to be one which provided a second-choice and therefore necessarily a second-rate form of education. "Adult education" was a flexible term; it was applied to courses and lectures in technical study, pottery making, cookery, woodworking, the appreciation of music, and many other subjects. These were worthy activities but they could hardly be considered "significant" or "substantial" on the level of higher education. Evening education suffered increasingly from the handicap of labels which seemed, in both the public and the academic mind, to establish limitations as well as limits.

In contrast, John P. Dyer in *Ivory Towers in the Market Place* reports that the one hundred members of the Association of University Evening Colleges use thirty-three different names. Most common, in order of frequency, are Evening Division, Evening College, and University College. Others are Intown College, Downtown College, College of Adult Education, School of General Studies, Community College, College of Special and Continuation Studies, and one which Mr. Dyer finds particularly interesting in its descriptive value—Twilight School.

In its early phases, evening education was regarded by most of those administering and teaching it as a continuation of secondary education. The content of many courses was simplified and diluted. While curricula might lead to degrees, they often were not directed in a systematic way toward the professional and humanistic growth and development of the student. Efforts were made to correlate and integrate courses, but the efforts frequently were incomplete or ineffectual.

Exploratory thinking among those concerned with evening education was accelerated in the years following World War II, when students wanting education of all kinds at all levels increased numerically at a rapid rate. Consideration was given to the objectives, new and old, of evening education, to the kinds and types, backgrounds and potentials of students to be served, and to methods of building curricula which would provide professional preparation and improvement and at the same time give the student perspective on his relation to the society and the culture of which he is a part. It was found that because evening education is not bound by long tradition and fixed patterns, any possibility could be examined and any feasible possibility could be undertaken. As a result, evening education of the present decade is not only more extensive than it was fifteen years ago but is much improved in quality and scope.

At Northeastern, the changes in evening education during the past fifteen years are accounted for by the trends of the period and by some special local conditions.

By the early 1940's, Northeastern had determined and established its position and role in the educational community of Boston, and it already had or had in prospect the facilities and equipment adequate to meet the new and larger needs. Northeastern was in all respects a flexible university, experienced in adapting itself to changing educational conditions. Finally, there was at the University personnel with interest and belief in evening education and the administrative and promotional ability needed to develop and conduct the kind of evening education called for in a new period.

In 1945, Albert E. Everett was made Dean of the School of Business and Director of the Evening Division. Dean Everett, a graduate of Northeastern, had become a member of the University faculty in 1927, as a Co-ordinator in the Department of Co-operative Work. In the years immediately preceding his appointment in 1945 he had been in charge of the Engineering, Science, and Management War Training program. In his new position, he worked on the development of the School of Business, while Donald H. MacKenzie took charge of Lincoln Institute.

Dean MacKenzie had been graduated from Northeastern in 1931 and had been associated with the University thereafter, as a teacher, an assistant in the Department of Student Activities, and in other administrative work. Under his direction Lincoln Institute was adapted to the post-war period. Courses were strengthened by the increase in class sessions from two hours to two and one-half, with a resultant substantial increase in the semester hours of credit required for a degree. Course content was upgraded and modernized, and basic programs were changed; curricula in electronics and in industrial engineering were added, and the aeronautics option in mechanical engineering was dropped.

These changes, in a time of increasing demand for specialized technical training, resulted in a consistent growth in the quality and enrollment of Lincoln Institute. Quality was reflected by enrollment, as students sought and found the evening study which satisfied their needs and interests. In the academic year 1944–1945, 367 students studied at Lincoln Institute, and were taught by a faculty of twenty-eight. In 1959–1960, the enrollment was 3966, and the faculty numbered 185.

After some changes and experiments, the Institute established its offerings as Chemistry, leading to the degree of Associate in Science; Civil, Electrical, Electronic, Industrial, and Mechanical Engineering, leading to the degree of Associate in Engineering; and an Engineering and Management program by which, with additional work in the School of Business, a student could earn the degree of Bachelor of Business Administration.

Students enrolled in these programs are men and women whose daily work is on technical and semi-technical jobs in a great diversity of companies, large and small, in the Greater Boston area. They continue their education in preparation for advancement in their work to more responsible and more difficult jobs, and each year more of them are sponsored financially, wholly or in part, by the companies for which they work.

The expansion of the School of Business during the past fifteen years has been even more marked than the growth of Lincoln Institute. The reasons are the industrial changes which have taken place in Massachusetts, coupled with Dean Everett's energetic administration and his policy of going out to the business community to determine the varying needs of different areas and industries and then constructing courses and groups of courses to meet these needs.

Under Dr. Everett's administration the School of Business was rebuilt to serve three distinct groups of students.

Degree candidates constituted the largest number of students in the School of Business. By way of eighteen professional programs leading to the degree of Bachelor of Business Administration they completed a series of Core Courses, for general orientation to business; Professional Courses, dealing with a field of specialization; and Liberal Arts courses, directed toward a view of man in relation to his culture, his society, and his universe. The total of the academic work represented 124 semester hours, in contrast to the forty-eight hours required by the original School of Commerce and Finance.

Many of the degree candidates came to the School of Business to complete a college education started elsewhere at an earlier time. A survey of the student body conducted in 1959 by Richard W. Bishop of the School of Business staff showed that of the 2,808 students who returned the survey questionnaire, 1,370 had previously attended seventy-eight New England colleges and 112 colleges in other parts of the country and abroad.

The second group of students enrolled in Institute programs, where they took courses dealing with such business areas as insurance, retailing, labor relations, and office management. These students accumulated credit toward a certificate or qualification for transfer to one of the degree programs.

Special students constituted a third group. They were working men and women, some of them college graduates with advanced degrees, who needed a special skill, such as drafting, or who wanted to study new and current developments in an area of previous study. They came to the School of Business for single courses or a series of related courses.

Since 1945, the work of the evening School of Business has been experimental and exploratory in many directions. From these efforts have come pioneer courses in job analysis and evaluation, transportation and traffic management, materials handling and, more recently, reliability engineering; early courses in statistical quality control led to the founding of the Boston Society of Quality Control.

Since 1954 an important adjunct of the School of Business has been the Bureau of Business and Industrial Training. The Bureau was an outgrowth of the Engineering, Science, and Management War Training program, a government-sponsored national effort to train workers as replacements of men who had gone into active war service and to prepare workers in war industries for more advanced technical jobs. Northeastern participated in the program from 1940 to 1945 and, largely through the work of Dr. Everett, developed a total of 135 special courses in mathematics, physics, drawing, chemistry, radio, industrial methods, time study, electronics, and similar subjects.

The industrial experience of World War II and the conditions of the post-war period established a general recognition of the need for special training of company personnel to meet local company problems. After some experimentation, the Bureau of Business and Industrial Training undertook to meet the need with both brief and extended courses, usually conducted at the company rather than on the campus and always courses prepared specifically for the occasion rather than courses from the regular curricula of the School of Business. By 1959 the Bureau was working with forty different New England companies, for some providing single courses in such subjects as letter writing or quality control, for others furnishing an extended program of training to prepare young company personnel for managerial work in future years.

The work of the Bureau was, in the usual sense, nonacademic, since the courses and groups of courses did not carry credit toward a degree. In contrast, the School of Business initiated in 1950 programs of study leading to the degree of

114

Master of Business Administration. This academic work attracted students who were interested in more knowledge of business and the professional advantage of an advanced degree and who were available for classroom work only in the evening.

Another evidence of the extension and improvement of evening education in the post-war decades is the changes that have taken place at Northeastern in evening study in liberal arts.

In 1938, Northeastern started a two-year pre-legal program in liberal arts, as preparation for entrance to schools of law. Two years later the program was extended in requirements to an Associate in Arts degree course which gave the student four choices: termination of collegiate study, pre-legal preparation, transfer to a day college of liberal arts at Northeastern or elsewhere, and transfer to the Northeastern School of Business. In 1953, a further extension of requirements established a program leading to the Bachelor of Arts degree.

X

STUDENT ACTIVITIES

The January 20, 1926, issue of the student newspaper *The Northeastern Tech* reported in its front page lead story:

"Professor Joseph Spear, since 1921 in charge of the Department of Student Activities, has submitted to Dean Ell his resignation as Director of Student Activities in order to devote his entire time to the Department of Mathematics of which he is chairman.

"When Professor Spear came to the school, student activities were almost non-existent. A paper, 'The Co-op,' was irregularly published, an occasional dance was held, and once in a while the classes held smokers. Under his direction, the musical activities of the school were initiated and developed. By devoted work, he gathered together a band; begged, borrowed, or bought instruments, training his raw recruits until they could present a creditable program. The orchestra, also, was started by him in much the same way. His enthusiasm, however, was not confined to musical activities. In March, 1920, he planned the still-remembered Degree Jubilee. . . . In the spring he had a large part in developing Field Day, now a Northeastern tradition."

This report, as well as the surviving records of the period, shows that during the 1920's extracurricular activities at Northeastern became a planned and significant part of the work of the young university. There was, however, background to this development, and a groundwork on which to build.

Student Activities

In October of 1916 a monthly student newspaper *The Co-op* made its first appearance. It was a small, four-page, three-column publication, and the first number announced that it had been started "through the efforts of Mr. Ell." In the same year local professional societies in Civil, Mechanical, Electrical, and Chemical Engineering were started; in later years these organizations and societies in other academic curricula became affiliated with regional and national societies.

In the spring of 1917 a senior annual *The Cauldron* was issued. It contained pictures of twenty seniors and a faculty of nineteen, and was dedicated to Hercules Geromanos, then Dean of the School of Engineering. It reported the activities of the year, including a Co-op Orchestra, a Student Council, a Co-op Glee Club, a Co-op Dance, and a Co-op Athletic Association.

A particularly interesting summary in this first yearbook reports the season of a basketball team, coached by Carl S. Ell and completing its season with six victories and five losses. The opponents were the Boston YMCA, Bridgewater Normal School, Rhode Island State Normal School, Massachusetts College of Pharmacy, Massachusetts Nautical Training School, Wentworth Institute, Watertown Community Club, and two games each with Fitchburg State Normal School and Boston University.

The war period following 1916–1917 curtailed student activities. *The Cauldron* did not appear again until 1921, but *The Co-op* continued to be published on a somewhat irregular basis. Fraternities entered the structure of activities during this interim period with the founding of Beta Gamma Epsilon and Alpha Kappa Sigma in 1919 and Eta Tau Nu in the next year.

Although Joseph Spear was not officially in charge of student activities until 1921, he was a dynamic force in that area immediately after his joining the faculty in 1919, following his war service and before that two years of teaching mathematics and German at the University of Maine. By 1920 Professor Spear had recruited and trained a vigorous band of eighteen members, including Edward S. Parsons '22 and Albert E. Everett '23.

The new Department of Student Activities of 1921 was made up of Divisions of Publications, Athletics, and Miscellaneous Activities; a Division of Music was added later. The department developed its own budget and financial control by way of a ten-dollar Student Activities Fee which was accepted by vote of the students and was later increased to fifteen dollars, also by vote of the students.

During Professor Spear's administration of activities the four divisions of the department added new activities and improved those that had already existed.

In publications, the student newspaper, which in 1920 had changed its name to *The Northeastern Tech*, expanded to a five-column page and increased its circulation from 600 to 1800 as the student body grew. *The Cauldron* reappeared in 1921 and has had a continuous life since that year. A student handbook or "Freshman Bible" was added to the annual publications.

The Division of Athletics took over direction of three sports, added three, and in 1924 established athletics on a University basis, with requirements for eligibility, letter awards, and other phases of intercollegiate competition.

From 1920 onward baseball and basketball were major sports, with regular scheduled seasons and coaching by successive members of the faculty. Track had a slightly earlier start. In 1919 a team made up of members of the classes of 1922 and 1923 carried out a limited but organized season. In the next year a team captained by Edward Parsons and Hjalmar Fundin was active, and in 1921, with Joseph W. Zeller as Coach of Track, this sport was firmly established. By 1925 it had developed sufficiently in status and participation to warrant the beginning of cross country as a separate varsity sport.

Wrestling was added to Northeastern sports in the 1920's but it did not become a permanent part of the program. There is also a record of swimming as an activity, though not as a recognized sport.

In the fall of 1922 soccer was started as a minor sport, and the new team had the satisfaction of winning its first game, with M.I.T. as opponent. The sport was launched and developed through the efforts of George Frost '24, a native of England who at Northeastern was captain of the first soccer team, captain and coach in the next year, and therefore referred to at the time as "the father of soccer at Northeastern." In 1926 soccer was made a major sport and it continued as an active and popular phase of the athletic program until 1933, when football was introduced.

The Division of Music included by 1925 a Band, Concert Orchestra, Glee Club, Banjo Club, Dance Orchestra, and Dramatic Club.

Miscellaneous Activities are recorded as Activities Mass Meetings, Field Day, the Rush, Student Council, and "many minor activities."

Field Day was an all-University outing initiated in 1910, developed to major proportions after 1920, and continued until the late 1930's, when the size of Northeastern made a family picnic impractical. On June days through those years, students, faculty members and their families, alumni, and friends gathered, regardless of weather, at Riverside Recreational Grounds in Weston for a day and evening of games and races, faculty-senior baseball, canoe tilting, tennis, golf, eating, dancing, and general conviviality.

The Freshman-Sophomore Rush was launched in 1919 by the class of 1922. It continued until 1932, when the Student Council, led by President John LaBelle '32, voted to abandon it because "it has outlived its usefulness."

In its heyday, the Rush was one of the non-academic high points of the Northeastern year. On a designated day, Division A freshmen and sophomores met in combat in the Fenway; in Division B they were forced to meet for less vigorous activities in the YMCA gymnasium. The Rush in the Fenway, near the Museum of Fine Arts, was always climaxed by a Pole Rush, with one class gathered around a twelve-foot greased pole on the top of which flew class colors, while the other class stormed the phalanx of students in an attempt to reach the top of the

119

pole and seize the colors; and a tug-of-war, for which the two classes were organized in line on opposite banks of the shallow and sluggish but well named Muddy River. Attendant exciting activities, in the years of the Rush, included various forms of psychological as well as physical warfare, most important the abduction of class presidents on the night before the critical day. The increasing size of both freshman and sophomore classes, the increasing number of abrasions, contusions, and other mishaps, and the increasing tendency of both classes to relieve at least a few of their opponents of their clothing in the Pole Rush led to the prohibitive action by the Student Council.

In 1920 the English High Club was organized, to bring together for social purposes the Northeastern students who had been graduated by that school. This was the first of a series of similar town, city, and regional clubs which flourished until the numbers involved made them unmanageable, while at the same time student interests and energies came to be centered in the collegiate activities at Northeastern. At the height of their popularity the clubs included Salem High, Brockton, Everett, Milford, Nutmeg State, Maine-Iacs, Lawrence, Empire State, Quincy, Haverhill, and Twin State.

In 1921 The Senate, an engineering honor society for students "high in scholarship and activities," was created by the joint initiative of Professors Joseph Spear and Philip Nash. A parallel society, Sigma Delta Epsilon, was formed in 1925 in the new College of Business Administration; later it became the Sigma Society. The Senate was, in later years, accepted as a chapter of the national engineering honor society Tau Beta Pi, and additional chapters of national societies in the College of Engineering were Eta Kappa Nu, for students of electrical engineering; and Pi Tau Sigma, for students of mechanical engineering. In 1937 The Academy was formed as the honor society of the College of Liberal Arts; a local chapter of Phi Alpha Theta, open to students of history, was established later. The most recent of the Northeastern units of national honor societies is a chapter of Kappa Iota Epsilon, formed by students of education.

A revised Student Council undertook student government in 1924, under one of the many constitutions that have been written and implemented through the decades of Northeastern activities. In the following year a Student Union was formed, with Milton J. Schlagenhauf as its first faculty adviser and with the stated purpose: "to broaden engineering education by lectures, trips, and religious activities."

All of these developments, as well as the "many minor activities," were instigated or promoted by Professor Spear. He encouraged an Inter-fraternity Council when there were only four fraternities at Northeastern, and in the interest of academic encouragement he was chairman of the first Board of Freshman Advisers, which consisted of five other members of the faculty.

The second Director of Student Activities, from 1926 to 1929, was Harold W. Melvin, who had joined the Northeastern faculty in 1920 and in the following year had been put in charge of the Department of English. In 1929 Professor Melvin became the University's first Dean of Students and at that time was succeeded in activities work by Edward S. Parsons, who continued for twenty-four years, with the later title of Director of Health, Physical Training, and Student Activities; in 1953 he left the department to become Business Manager of the University. Professor Parsons represented Northeastern in numerous regional and national athletic organizations, including a term as district Vice President of the National Collegiate Athletic Association, as a member of the NCAA Council, and on several committees of the United States Olympic Association.

After 1953 a period of two years with a division of athletics and a division of student activities was followed by a reunited department with Herbert W. Gallagher '35 as Director and Charles E. Kitchin as Associate Director. In 1960, as one phase of the University reorganization initiated by President Knowles, the complex area of athletics and non-athletic activities was again divided; Professor Gallagher became Director of Health and Athletics, Professor Kitchin was made Director of Student Activities, and the general supervision of the non-athletic program was added to the administration of the Dean of Students.

Under the guidance of this succession of men, student activities at Northeastern have gone through periods of experimentation and varying vitality, but consistent growth in number and variety as the student body grew in size and as the tastes and interests of successive generations of college students changed. "Student Activities Hours," Tuesday and Thursday from twelve to two, were established to provide definite periods for athletic practice, rehearsals, club meetings, and general assemblies. This provision, together with the development of an advisory system whereby a member of the faculty worked with each organized and recognized student group, was designed to offset the limitations of "campus life" from which any urban university suffers, and to encourage development and self-realization among students through activity and leadership in small groups. The result has been a flexible program, adapted not only through the decades but from year to year to student-motivated interests and desires.

In dramatics, for example, the early and somewhat half-hearted clubs were followed by a series of annual all-University shows from 1924 to 1934. Six were original musical comedies in which were united the creative and dramatic talents of students, various members of the faculty including Professor Melvin, and professional coaches brought in for the occasion. With sprightly and topical titles *Listenin In, Are You My Wife?, The Rajah of Kashmir, Yes, Yes, Siam,* and *Top o' the World,* the series came to an end and a climax with *Banned in Boston,* a large production involving a cast of seventy-five, an orchestra of fifty pieces, a puppet prologue, and a gala presentation in the Arlington Theatre; this production was developed and directed by Trentwell Mason White, then a member of the Department of English, and in later years, until his death, President of Leslie College.

122

Student Activities

A new Dramatic Club was formed in 1934 and functioned for several years under the handicaps of meager facilities and the necessity of borrowing girls from neighboring colleges for plays with mixed casts. After the arrival of co-eds on campus and the building of Alumni Auditorium, the club became the Silver Masque and under the direction of Eugene J. Blackman, member of the Department of English and in 1959 head of the new Department of Drama, Speech, and Music, developed a substantial and effective program of three plays and one musical production during each academic year. The Silver Masque has presented such outstanding plays and musicals as *The Barretts of Wimpole Street, Ah, Wilderness, All My Sons, Pygmalion, A View From the Bridge, Born Yesterday, Dark of the Moon, Finian's Rainbow, Oklahoma, South Pacific, Carousel,* and *Fanny.*

Two major sports were added to the athletic structure. Hockey was initiated through the promotional activity of H. Nelson Raymond '28, who in his senior year circulated petitions and built up student interest in the sport. The first season was 1929–1930 with Mr. Raymond as coach. Thereafter, in spite of difficulties in scheduling practice sessions, hockey became one of the most successful Northeastern sports. Another alumnus important to its development was Herbert Gallagher, a brilliant player as an undergraduate and later coach of hockey for a total of fifteen seasons.

Football was introduced by administrative decision rather than student initiative. After a year of freshman games with junior colleges and other freshman teams, the first varsity season, 1933, consisted of games with St. Anselm's College, St. Michael's College, Colby College, Arnold College, and Norwich University. Alfred M. McCoy was coach of the freshman team and of the first four varsity teams.

By 1935 the athletic activities of Northeastern had been developed to the inter-collegiate status of membership by the University in the New England Intercollegiate Amateur Athletic Association, the Association of New England Colleges for

Conference on Athletics, the New England Association of the Amateur Athletics Union, the Intercollegiate Association of Amateur Athletes of America, the National Collegiate Athletic Association, and the United States Olympic Association. When the Eastern College Athletic Conference was formed in 1947, Northeastern was one of the charter members.

As an adjunct to athletics a club called the Fore Paw Key was organized in 1929 to promote school spirit, student support of athletics, and relations with visiting teams and students. Among its contributions to campus life was the launching of a traditional event, the Football Dance, in 1934. Because of the curtailment of college athletics during the war years, the Fore Paw Key ceased to function, but it was reactivated in 1948 as the Husky Key to carry on, under different conditions and with different activities, the purpose of the original organization.

The Student Union expanded and adapted its functions, particularly after Charles W. Havice became its adviser in 1927. Such projects as noon-hour programs, an annual drive for contributions to missionary work in South Africa, walking tours in historic Boston, and overnight camping as a part of freshman orientation were conducted as long as they contributed to the well-being and community college life of students. Later efforts were concentrated in the two areas of co-operative projects with and service to other student groups on campus, and volunteer social service work at settlement houses, hospitals, the Braille Press, and community centers.

Certainly the most vital single contribution of the Student Union to the life of Northeastern has been the weekly Chapel services. In October of 1927 the first service was held in the church then known as the Church of the Messiah, on the corner of Gainsborough and St. Stephen Streets; President Frank Palmer Speare was the speaker and the attendance was about two hundred students and faculty. In the following year and for two years thereafter the services were held in Repertory Hall, a part of the Repertory Theater on Huntington Avenue. Later Chapel homes were a room in the Huntington Building and then in Richards Hall. The Student Center was planned and built to contain a well appointed Chapel, a suitable setting for the weekly services.

In 1940 Dr. Havice was made Dean of Chapel and at that time gave up direct guidance of the Student Union. Chapel services continued in the pattern which he had established in 1927—non-denominational worship periods at which visiting representatives of different faiths gave ethical and moral talks to students and faculty. As the faculty grew in size and in wisdom through age, Dean Havice invited members of that group to the Chapel pulpit, alternating with clergymen of the Boston area. A Chapel Choir was developed by Laurence F. Cleveland of the Department of Electrical Engineering to become a valuable part of the services. Professor Cleveland has had a long association with Northeastern Chapel and made an unusual contribution by building, in 1940, an electronic organ which was used until the construction of the Student Center.

The Bacon Memorial Chapel, the gift to Northeastern of Chandler & Company and dedicated to the memory of Charles F. Bacon, has become a source of varied and deep associations and values for many Northeastern people. The Chapel organ was dedicated by the Student Union to the memory of Miss Eva Kinnear, sister of Mrs. Carl Ell, who for several years before her death in 1932 was secretary, devoted worker, and friendly counselor to the Student Union. In recent years the Chapel has been the scene of the weddings of students and alumni, and of the baptism of children of Northeastern parentage. In some instances Dean Havice has performed both the marriage and baptism ceremonies for these young families.

For a brief period extracurricular activities at Northeastern moved in two parallel lines. The students in the College of Business Administration, starting in 1922, felt the independence and obligation of a new school in which they were pioneer citizens. Consequently they established their own organizations, including a Student Union, Student Council, dramatic club, orchestra, and a newspaper called *The Bulletin*. In 1926 the first graduating seniors, sixteen in number, produced *The Administrator*, a class yearbook. Parallel activities proved to be impractical, however, and in the next few years all organizations were combined. *The Bulletin* fused with *The Tech* to become *The Northeastern News* in February of 1926, and after three issues *The Administrator* was merged with *The Cauldron*.

Representative of the increasing diversity of student interests are the three widely different organizations: the Rifle Club, started in 1930 with G. Raymond Fennell as its first coach, and the basis of later rifle teams and riflery as a minor sport; the International Relations Club of 1932 with Roger S. Hamilton as its first adviser; and the Husky Highlighters, formed in 1948 by Dean Melvin for noontime broadcasts within the University of campus news, announcements, and some entertainment.

Some social functions and planned organizations came into being to meet a current wave of interest and enthusiasm, and later disappeared from the scene because, like the Freshman-Sophomore Rush, they had outlived their usefulness. Some were annual all-University affairs like the Minstrel Show and Spring Concert and later the Mid-winter Concert and Dance, the Round-up of students, faculty, and friends held in the Boston City Club, and Home Folks' Day conducted for four successive years by the first students of the College of Business Administration.

In 1922 Frank Palmer Speare founded the Delta Society "to develop school spirit, character, and spiritual values." The Class of 1925 started the Sagitta Society of Sophomores "to promote inter-divisional activity and to enforce freshman rules." A Flying Club of 1927, guided by Professor Nightingale, was active for several years before it languished because of lack of equipment in which to do actual flying. A foreshadowing of later postwar periods is the Federal Board Club of 1924, made up of forty-one veterans of World War I "who are receiving governmental aid in their education at Northeastern University."

Student Activities

Although in many respects the early periods of student activities and student life at Northeastern were simple and by later standards unsophisticated, there are some indications of a surprising degree of elegance and precision of decorum. In the fall of 1921 *The Tech* approved editorially of the presence of faculty guests at an Alpha Kappa Sigma informal dance in informal dress; the faculty thereby, said the editorial, "departed from an ancient custom and established a precedent." Another illustration of the exactitude of the early years is the instructions appearing in *The Tech* in 1920: "The members of the school who are wearing the school pin will please be careful to see that the arrow points to the northeast. When a person is upright, north is directly over the head, and east is to the left."

Through the years the common and basic interests of students have been satisfied by a growth of stable and permanent activities.

The two original fraternities, Alpha Kappa Sigma and Beta Gamma Epsilon, both founded in 1919, were later augmented by other local fraternal groups—Nu Epsilon Zeta, 1921; Sigma Kappa Psi, 1921; Kappa Zeta Phi, 1924; Phi Beta Alpha, 1924; Phi Gamma Pi, 1924; Sigma Phi Alpha, 1924; Gamma Phi Kappa, 1925; Phi Alpha Rho, 1960. Three fraternities—Eta Tau Nu, founded in 1920, and Sigma Delta and Iota Sigma, founded in 1925—relinquished their charters in later years. An Interfraternity Council built up through the years a spirit of unity and co-operation among the fraternities. Especially in the years after 1954, when Professor William H. Reynolds of the Department of English took over advisorship, the IFC showed stability and originality in maintaining and initiating projects and events. The fraternity scholarship shield, originated in 1929, was continued; interfraternity activity in bowling, basketball, and softball was encouraged and supervised; in co-operation with the Husky Key, the IFC worked to promote the Northeastern sports program; it conducted an annual Christmas party for children patients in Boston City Hospital; and at the Uni-

127

Origin and Development of Northeastern University

versity Convocation of October, 1959, the IFC presented to President Knowles the first Northeastern flag, which the IFC had designed and purchased as a contribution to the University and the establishment of a new symbolic tradition.

As women students increased in numbers, they formed two general social societies—Omega Sigma in 1944 and Gamma Delta in 1958.

Special sports interests were developed in the Hus-Skiers and the Yacht Club, with the result that skiing and yachting were accepted as minor sports.

The Politics Club, Art Club, Debating Society, and several organizations open only to students in ROTC illustrate the diversity of student activities in the large university which Northeastern became.

A postgraduate interest in Northeastern activities and a desire to retain the associations developed in college led to the formation of alumni groups among former members of the Silver Masque and *The News*, and the Varsity Club, made up of alumni who were letter men in Northeastern sports.

Since 1926 the mascot symbol of Northeastern activities in general and sports in particular has been the Siberian Eskimo dog. No other non-academic element in Northeastern's history has drawn to itself so much color and romance and, on the other hand, so many complications and crises.

In 1926 it became evident to various people at the University, including Edward R. Place, then director of the Publicity Department, that Northeastern athletic teams needed a mascot and a name for identification of Northeastern sports in the public mind. A suggestion contest conducted by *The News* resulted in a variety of possibilities—"everything from ant to elephant." The bee was seriously considered, until someone foresaw the possibility of Northeastern athletic defeats being reported on sports pages under the headline "NU Bees Stung Again." The name "Husky" was chosen.

Through the efforts of Dean Ell, including a winter visit to Poland Springs, Maine, Leonard Seppala gave to the University its first mascot, King Husky I. Mr. Seppala was at that time a breeder and racer of Siberian dogs, and internationally known as the hero of a sled-dog emergency run to Nome to carry serum to a stricken city.

The new mascot arrived in Boston on March 9, 1927. He was met at North Station and there a parade formed consisting of 1200 students, a police escort, the Northeastern Band, and in central position a float on which rode the King, Mr. Seppala, and six Northeastern secretaries; three of the secretaries were known to Northeastern students in later years as Mrs. Mildred Garfield, Mrs. Jessie Rhodes, and Mrs. Mary Reynolds.

The New York *Times* considered the progress of the parade sufficiently newsworthy to report, in part:

"With several hundred students grouped on the steps of the Boston University business administration building and scores more jamming every window overlooking Boylston Street, the demonstration began right after the mounted police detail leading the parade had passed.

"Frozen snow was showered on the band and succeeding sections of the parade were pelted with missiles. Women and girl spectators received much that was badly thrown, hats and coats being spoiled by broken eggs. The windshield of a passing motor car was broken by a piece of ice.

"Each volley was countered by the marching students with a cheer for Boston University, and they kept on marching. Several policemen went into the college building and confiscated crates of eggs and vegetables before they could be utilized. When the Northeastern boys took the punishment jokingly and refused to retaliate, several Boston University students tried to stop the missile throwing by calling for cheers for Northeastern."

The aftermath of this stimulating episode was a renewal of amicable relations between the students of the two universities. On March 17 the new mascot's first birthday was celebrated at Northeastern, and among the greetings was a card measuring three feet by five feet from the students of Boston University;

129

later in the spring King Husky appeared as a guest of honor at a Boston University mass meeting.

King Husky I was Northeastern's mascot until March of 1941. In that period of fourteen years he made frequent appearances at student gatherings, won prizes at the Eastern Dog Show, and in many respects lived up to his royal name and significant position. At the same time, he created problems for Dr. Ell, who during most of the period housed the mascot in Newton and on Cape Cod; King Husky ate well and extensively, on two occasions was at liberty and lost for several days, and on the Cape for summer vacation varied his confined life by ranging the countryside and causing expensive damage in a poultry farm.

The first mascot was followed by Queen Husky I, the gift to the University of Mr. and Mrs. Milton Seeley, proprietors of the Chinook Kennels at Wonalancet, New Hampshire. The Queen, welcomed to the University not only by the students but by greetings from the Bates Bobcat, the Bowdoin Polar Bear, the Colby Mule, the University of Maine Black Bear, and Danny, the Boston University mascot, died at the early age of six months.

The later succession was King Husky II, presented to the University in 1942 by Mr. and Mrs. Seeley; King Husky III in 1952, also from the Chinook Kennels; and King Husky IV, who made a guest appearance at the University in February, 1958, accompanied by Mrs. Eva Seeley.

By 1958 the difficulties of maintaining a living mascot in Boston, under climatic conditions alien to the Siberian Husky, coupled with complications arising from the deaths of successive members of the royal line, culminated in a review of policy. Through agreement of the Student Council, the Faculty Committee on Student Activities, and the Executive Council of the University, a new phase of symbolism was established in 1959. Students conducted a fund-raising campaign for creating a bronze statue of King Husky I, and the Executive Council agreed to duplicate the amount raised by student solicitation.

Student Activities

In future years the spirit of King Husky I—stated in 1927 by President Speare as "endurance, determination, intelligence, recognition of leadership and a willingness to enter wholeheartedly into teamwork"—will be perpetuated by a permanent, though inanimate, symbol.

XI

THE STUDENT IN AFTER YEARS

Since early in the century, when in 1902 and 1903 a group of forty-two men completed the curriculum of the School of Law, over 20,000 men and women have become alumni of Northeastern. Since the late 1920's, this growing body of graduates has contributed substantially to the present status and stature of the University.

The relationship has been a reciprocal one. As alumni have reached positions of significance in all areas of business, the professions, and the academic world, they have created in the public mind an increasing awareness of Northeastern and its accomplishment. As the University itself has developed, alumni have benefited from public recognition and acceptance of a young but major university in action.

It is to the credit of Northeastern alumni that early efforts toward organized activities were self-imposed. For a period of ten years, groups were formed through the interest and energy of a few graduates; some of these groups were short-lived, but they laid the groundwork for later developments.

In 1915, one hundred graduates of the School of Commerce and Finance met as an Association "mainly for social purposes." In 1919, "former members of the Day Division" set up a social organization with Roland G. Porter '18 as temporary Chairman. This group held a "First Annual Banquet" at the Parker House and elected John R. Leighton '14 as President. The Annual Banquet later became the "Fall Dinner" and still later "Homecoming Day," and has been a continuous annual event since 1919. In recent years Homecoming Day has become a gala fusion of undergraduate and alumni activities—a football game, with a parade of floats and the crowning of a campus Beauty Queen; an Alumni dinner; and the presentation of a play by the Silver Masque.

The Northeastern University Club of Boston was organized in 1922 with a membership of one hundred, but it disappeared from the records soon thereafter. In 1924 the class of that year in the School of Law organized a Law School Alumni Association with Asa S. Allen as President.

Against the background of these spontaneous and well-intentioned activities a long process of organization and consolidation was initiated by the appointment in 1927 of William C. White as the first Alumni Secretary. During the next three years he established the basis of the future cementing of relations between alumni and the University.

The first organized class reunion, that of the Class of 1922, took place in 1927. In the same year *The Northeastern Alumni Bulletin* made its first appearance. In later years, with some brief periods of inactivity along the way, the *Bulletin* became *The Nor'easter* and in 1945 a quarterly magazine, *The Northeastern Alumnus*. The alumni of the College of Engineering and the College of Business Administration were united in one organization in 1928, with William M. Parsons '24 as President.

When William White was made Secretary of the Day Division faculty in 1929, he was succeeded in alumni work by Rudolf O. Oberg '26, who became Alumni Secretary of the Day Colleges. By 1943 his work had become so extensive that an Alumni Office was created, and he was appointed Director of Alumni Relations.

In that year the Alumni Fund was organized as the first consistent appeal to graduates for financial contributions to their University, although an Endowment Campaign had been conducted as early as 1928, and alumni had been solicited in 1938 for funds for the building of Richards Hall.

The Alumni Fund became an annual project, each year with a special objective determined by the Alumni Fund Committee, in consultation with the President of the University. Through the years these objectives have been directed mainly toward the Northeastern building program—the underwriting of the cost of Alumni Auditorium, contributions to the Library, equipment for the Physical Education Center. Other major enterprises have been a $100,000 Alumni Faculty Salary Endowment Fund, and an Alumni Scholarship Fund of the same amount.

Northeastern alumni were solidified by the formation of the Alumni Federation in 1946. With Robert Bruce '14 as its first Chairman, the Federation coordinated the activities and interests of graduates of the Day Colleges, the School of Law, and the School of Business. The Federation proved its effectiveness in forming what Dr. Ell called "one united voice," through the representatives of schools and colleges who constitute the structure of the Federation.

Alumni participation in vital matters of University policy has increased as the alumni have grown in numbers, age, and willingness to contribute their abilities, judgment, and specialized knowledge. In 1937, by vote of the University Corporation, the President of the Alumni Association became a member of the Corporation by virtue of his office. In 1952 the Corporation established a plan of Alumni Term Members; by this plan four alumni are added to the Corporation each year for four-year terms, with the result that there always are sixteen alumni term members serving as members of the body. Since 1956 at least one alumnus has been elected each year to the Corporation as a regular member.

In recognition of distinguished accomplishment in some area of professional work and in citizenship, the University has included in the group of honorary degree recipients at June commencements since 1952 one member or more of the alumni body.

The Student in After Years

Before 1952, five alumni had received honorary degrees—Sanford Bates '06 in 1937, Horace T. Cahill '18 in 1940, John P. Higgins '27 in 1940, Cyrus S. Ching '12 in 1946, and Frederick J. Dillon '23 in 1950. All of these men were graduates of the Northeastern School of Law, and from the University received the honorary degree of Doctor of Laws.

Since 1952, the alumni honored by the University have been the following, listed here with the positions they held at the time of the conferring of the degree:

1952—William C. White '25, Director of Day Colleges of Northeastern University, Doctor of Engineering

1953—George Hansen '18, President of Chandler & Company, Doctor of Laws

1954—J. Harold Stewart '18, Partner in the firm of Stewart, Watts & Bollong, Doctor of Commercial Science

1955—Charles N. Kimball '31, President, Midwest Research Institute, Doctor of Engineering

1955—Frank L. Flood '22, Senior Partner, Metcalf and Eddy, Doctor of Engineering

1956—Albert E. Everett '23, Director of the Evening Division and Dean of the School of Business, Northeastern University, Doctor of Commercial Science

1957—John L. Burns '30, President of the Radio Corporation of America, Doctor of Business Administration

1958—Arthur J. Pierce '32, Brigadier General, of the United States Air Force, Doctor of Laws

1959—William T. Alexander '26, Dean of the College of Engineering at Northeastern University, Doctor of Engineering

1960—Right Reverend Robert J. Sennott '32, Chancellor, Archdiocese of Boston, Doctor of Civil Law

William E. R. Sullivan '28, Brigadier General, United States Army, President, U. S. Army Chemical Corps Board, Doctor of Science

Following the tradition of American colleges, the Alumni Office promoted regional alumni clubs. In New York a group was organized by William White in 1927. The Connecticut

Club was formed in 1929. Eventually there were twenty-one Northeastern alumni clubs within the bounds of the country from Maine to California, as well as an unofficial club which holds an annual winter vacation session on a semi-tropical island. Some clubs have been large and some small, and some have passed through fluctuating periods of activity; but all have continued to be focal points of common interest in social functions, visits by representatives of the University, and a continuity of alumni support for the University.

As an encouragement to undergraduates, the Alumni Council started in 1947 the Senior Award for Professional Promise. Richard Newcomb of the College of Engineering was the first winner; in later years the Award was extended to include a senior from each of the four Day Colleges.

As a service to alumni, the University appointed in 1956 Thomas J. McEneaney '52 as Senior and Alumni Placement Officer. In addition to arranging recruitment visits and other interviews with seniors by industrial representatives, Mr. McEneaney works with several hundred alumni each year, referring them to job opportunities which he has on file and in many instances providing direct or indirect vocational counseling. The two large categories of alumni who consult Mr. McEneaney are recent graduates who have completed a term of service in the armed forces, and alumni who have become established professionally in other parts of the country but want to return to New England. The diversity of this service to alumni is illustrated by the placement of a member of the Class of 1917 who, upon retiring from a successful career, wanted to continue to use his ability and experience in a new but less demanding position.

From many points of view the most ambitious and at the same time appealing single project carried out by Northeastern alumni was the tribute in 1958–1959 to Dr. Ell, on the occasion of his retirement from the Presidency. The Alumni Day program in June was attended by eight hundred graduates and friends and included the unveiling of the inscription on the

The Student in After Years

Carl Stephens Ell Student Center Building, a reception to Dr. and Mrs. Ell, a dinner at which William C. White '25 and Gardner A. Caverly '34 were the speakers, and a deluge of greetings and gifts from alumni in all parts of the United States and in foreign countries. The gifts sent to Dr. and Mrs. Ell included such varied items as rice bowls from Japan and a living redwood tree from California. In September, as an aftermath to the June meeting, the Alumni Carl Stephens Ell Scholarship Fund of $100,000 was presented to the University.

The fact that Mrs. Ell shared conspicuously in this tribute from the alumni reflects the appreciation of all Northeastern people of the contribution which the wife of the second President made to the University.

In 1913 Miss Etta Kinnear became Mrs. Carl Ell, and thereafter, as Dr. Ell moved from one position to another in the development of Northeastern, she assumed increasing status and responsibility. Her natural warmth of personality and real concern for people led her to know intimately the faculty family. At scores of student affairs, ranging from football games to formal dances, Mrs. Ell was a figure of dignity and graciousness, another symbol of the spirit of Northeastern.

Mrs. Ell founded, in 1940, the Northeastern University Faculty Wives, an organization which since that time has not only held its own educational and social meetings but has provided scholarships for girl students and special gifts to the University. Mrs. Ell was President of the group from 1940 to 1943, and Honorary President until 1960.

In the local and the larger community Mrs. Ell has been a worker and a directive force in social service organizations in the city of Newton, in the Massachusetts Council of Churches, and in local and national committees of the Methodist Church.

The 1959 *Cauldron*, dedicated to Dr. Ell on his retirement from the Presidency of the University, carried in the dedicatory section a picture of Mrs. Ell and the following poetic statement by Michael Murphy of the Class of 1959—

The night drifts down on quiet wings;
Invisible forces move the Earth.
No mountain is, and no bird sings
But something underneath, behind,
Supports its being, tells its worth
Though all the world be blind.

During the early months of 1960, a committee of the Alumni Federation drafted a proposed All-University Alumni Constitution, to coordinate alumni activities with other administrative changes then taking place at the University. The purposes of the new constitution were stated to be: to promote the welfare of Northeastern University, to establish a mutually beneficial relationship between Northeastern University and its alumni, and to perpetuate fellowship among members of the Association.

By the provisions of the constitution all alumni were brought together under one Association, headed by a President, senior Vice President, and an Executive Committee. Lines of alumni work were established under the direction of four Vice Presidents, in charge of Alumni Fund, Alumni Affairs, Alumni Clubs, and Alumni Class Council. A new position, Director of Alumni Fund, was created. This officer, together with the Director of Alumni Relations and the Director of Development, is related directly to the President of the University, coordinating all phases of alumni relations, those sponsored by the University and those originating in the work of the elected officers of the Alumni Association. The new constitution recognized all constituent college groups of alumni, but within the structure and under the general direction of an All-University Alumni Association. This basic change in organization should result in a more effective and efficient program of alumni relations, and a closer relationship between the alumni and their University.

The cumulative accomplishment of Northeastern alumni directed toward the best interests of their alma mater has been accounted for by their growing recognition of a debt of the past and a genuine concern for the present and the future. At

138

the Inaugural Dinner of President Knowles in September, 1959, George C. Thompson '30, Chairman of the Alumni Federation, said, "I not only bring the greetings of my fellow alumni to Dr. Knowles, but also pledge the support of Northeastern's alumni in all projects that will make Northeastern University an ever greater institute of learning."

The promotion and direction of this feeling of identity with Northeastern among its alumni has for the past thirty years been the work of Rudolf Oberg. With distinguished service and assistance from Miss Marjorie King, Chief Secretary of the Alumni Office since 1945, he has established patterns of attitude and action unusual among the alumni of colleges which have a history of little more than half a century.

XII

WARS AND THE ARMED FORCES

When, on April 6, 1917, the United States declared that a state of war existed between itself and Germany, Northeastern was completing its first year as an incorporated college, and the inauguration of President Speare had taken place seven days before the declaration of war.

The tense, unsettled conditions of the war that was to end all wars provided an inauspicious setting for a small and struggling school of engineering. By the spring of 1918 the United States was prepared to send to Europe 120,000 troops every month. All of the energies of the American people were turned to what Woodrow Wilson called "Force, Force, to the utmost, Force without stint or limit, the righteous and triumphant Force which shall now make Right the law of the world, and cast every selfish dominion down in the dust."

During the summer vacation of 1917 Carl S. Ell went to Washington for a brief period of government work in structural design, and then to Albany for a special assignment with the New York Department of Health, for which he had done consulting work in 1913 and 1914. He returned to Northeastern for the opening of the school year and in mid-September became Dean of the School of Co-operative Engineering.

The annual report of the Boston YMCA for 1917–1918 summarized the Association's war program. As that program affected Northeastern, the report said, "The United States

Government has taken over our School of Co-operative Engineering as an S.A.T.C. Unit. Barracks for two hundred and fifty men are being constructed on the tennis courts; a fully equipped mess house is in progress for erection. Four officers under the command of Lieutenant A. Gordon Merry have already arrived. . . . The faculty of the school has been nearly doubled. . . . the school goes under military control October 1st."

The "regular War Program," designed "to prepare men so that they may go to camp ready for promotion," was described in the report as consisting of twenty-one courses, mainly technical but including Foreign Trade, Personal Development for Wartime Needs, Military French, and Typewriting. Airplane Mechanics was proving to be the most popular course, and the report referred to an engine laboratory and testing shed, and the use of a large area of the Boston Elevated Railway land near the YMCA for the possible construction of a hangar.

These activities and preparations were carried forward during the summer and fall of 1918. The actual functioning of the military unit was for only a brief period. A first-hand view of the period is given by Edward Parsons, who entered Northeastern as a freshman in September of 1918. After registration, all students were sent home for two weeks; when they returned, the barracks were in place on land now occupied by Dodge Library, and were partially equipped. Professor Parsons acted as chief bugler of the military unit and with other students then at Northeastern served a two-month Army period. After the end of the war on November 11 they were again sent home; when they returned, the barracks had disappeared and in December the students were discharged from the Army and returned to civilian academic life.

In two other areas Northeastern made educational contributions to World War I.

The 1917–1918 report of the Boston YMCA states: "The Huntington Preparatory School is offering to accomplish four years' work in two, two years' work in one, and six months' work in three in preparing men to enter the colleges and

141

thereby increase the available supply of men for the Officers' Training Camps. Over one hundred boys and young men have entered with this express purpose in mind."

The records of the Automobile School of this period indicate, though vaguely, that special brief courses in automobile driving and maintenance were set up for both men and women.

The outbreak of World War II and the six years of war that followed affected Northeastern as they affected all American colleges and universities. It was a period of constant adjustment and readjustment to the demands of total war.

Special programs and military reserve units continued through most of the war years. The Civilian Pilot Training Program was started at Northeastern in 1939; in following years, reserve groups of the Army, Navy, and Marines enabled many students to complete their college education before entering active service. On the other hand, the National Youth Administration, initiated by the federal government during the depression years, ended its ten-year program in 1942–1943. Northeastern played a conspicuous and active part in the Engineering, Science, and Management War Training program from 1940 to 1945 and thereby prepared for the later work of the Evening Division Bureau of Business and Industrial Training.

In June, 1942, the University introduced an intricate but helpful program of acceleration. By its provisions a student on the Co-operative Plan could complete his requirements for a degree eighteen months before his normal time of graduation, and by full-time study could increase the time saving to two years. Acceleration necessitated a twelve-month academic year, with two weeks of vacation for faculty and staff. It resulted in commencements in both June and December through 1943 to 1946, war degrees granted to seniors who had completed more than half of their last year of academic work, and a redistribution of class numerals which baffled the students involved and caused the Alumni Office extensive work of further redistribution in the post-war years.

By war-time expediences many students were carried through

142

to the completion of their undergraduate study. Many others were drafted. Most affected were the Day Colleges of Liberal Arts, which in 1940 had an enrollment of 503 and in 1943, 268; and the College of Business Administration, which dropped from a 1940 enrollment of 664 to a 1943 enrollment of 99. In the academic year 1943–1944, thirty-three members of the faculty were on military leave of absence.

In August, 1943, the War Department, after inspection and approval, authorized the establishment at Northeastern of a unit of the Army Specialized Training Program. In December, 350 ASTP students arrived on campus; the University in the meantime had prepared for their arrival by setting up living quarters on Hemenway Street, allocating members of the faculty to ASTP teaching, and implementing the courses called for by the special Army curriculum.

The three-month session of ASTP was an unusual experience for Northeastern but in many respects a satisfying experience. The young men, most of them former students in other colleges, provided rewarding classroom work for the faculty, some of whom found the military atmosphere and discipline foreign to their past teaching. Students from homes and colleges in other parts of the country enjoyed a brief period of living in New England, and built up associations at Northeastern, in the city of Boston, and in faculty homes. In February, 1944, Secretary of War Stimpson announced the discontinuance of ASTP except in limited areas. Early in March the Northeastern unit left Boston for special combat training; thereafter they participated in the Battle of the Bulge, where many of them were casualties and fatalities.

In the academic year 1944–1945, 267 veterans of World War II were enrolled at Northeastern. In 1950–1951 the veterans numbered 6990, or fifty-three per cent of the total enrollment of the University.

During this post-war period, another program of acceleration was carried out, enabling returned students to complete as soon as possible the education which had been interrupted by war service. The Day Division Class of 1950, for example, was graduated in three sections, each with its own commencement, social activities, and class yearbook, but all within a calendar year.

By 1952–1953, veterans of the Korean War were returning to or entering Northeastern; in the following year the registration of all colleges showed 1900 veterans of World War II and 2100 veterans of the Korean War. In this year a Veterans' Guidance Center was established by the University to work with students and government agencies.

The contribution of Northeastern to the two mid-century wars is incalculable. Alumni known to have been active in World War II totaled 5520; 241 Northeastern men lost their lives in the same war. Above and beyond such statistical evidence of the participation of Northeastern men, and the adaptation of the work of the University to the educational necessities of war years, is the inestimable contribution of Northeastern individuals and groups to the network of sustained human relationships which helped to make possible the completion of active warfare. One illustration, but cogent because of its continuing organized activity, is the work of *Husky Plus*, under the direction of Dean of Students Harold Melvin.

Husky Plus was a group of students enlisted by Dean Melvin to maintain correspondence with Northeastern men in military service during World War II. When letters from students gone to war reached such proportions that Dean Melvin could not answer them individually, he started a University letter, giving Northeastern and Boston news, reports of changes in military rank of former students, current addresses of Northeastern military personnel, a list of visits to the University by servicemen on leave, and always a message of greeting and encouragement from the Dean. The letter grew to extensive proportions and the later numbers were prepared by offset printing to include pictures. *Husky Plus*, so named by Dean Melvin because a group of students volunteered to do an extra job in the interest of their University, addressed, stamped, and mailed over 1200 copies of the letters sent out during the last months of the war. Casualties and fatalities were not mentioned until a final letter after the close of hostilities, when all that had been reported to the University were listed.

A similar letter from Dean Melvin was sent to servicemen in the Korean War.

The deep personal concern of Harold Melvin for students and alumni in war service as well as the gratitude of the University of which he was Dean was expressed in his tribute given at the Gold Star Memorial Service in Alumni Auditorium on June 18, 1948:

Remembering

Remembering the boys who have not returned,
Remembering their faces and what they said,
Remembering their books on tables at home,
The skis and fishing rods against the wall,
Remembering the cemeteries across the sea,
Boys buried in salt water and boys who died in camps,
Remembering the boys who have not come back,
What shall we say? Say this: "We who went away
And now are back remember you."
Or say: "We who waited at home for your return
Remember you." Say this: "That now
In lilac time, the Remembering Day of our Nation,
We are remembering. We are grateful to you,
—Not names upon a wall but in the heart—
Each of you—boys whom we know, remember, and miss.
So, inadequately, in the only way we can,
We pay our respect to you who gave so much,
Remembering you—we here, now, returned—
Giving this evening and this moment to you,
Standing silent, remembering . . .

In 1950, while veterans of World War II constituted more than half of the student population of Northeastern, mobilization for the war in Korea began to affect the plans and expectations of both high school students and college undergraduates. At Northeastern the establishment of an Army Reserve Officers' Training Corps stabilized student enrollment and introduced a new element into the operation, development, and history of Northeastern.

By order of the Secretary of the Army, effective April 1, 1951, two ROTC units—Corps of Engineers and Signal Corps—were authorized. The first Army officer to arrive on campus, in May, was Captain William H. Chestnut, a combat veteran and a graduate of the University of Buffalo. Working with Professor G. Raymond Fennell, who acted temporarily as Military Property Custodian, Captain Chestnut prepared for the arrival of the authorized personnel of seven officers and ten enlisted men, supplemented by a civilian typist and a University-employed supply clerk.

The ROTC unit was activated in September of 1951 under the command of Colonel Howard E. Price, a veteran of active service in Europe and Korea who came to Northeastern from North Carolina State College where he had been Assistant PMST.

Student enrollment in the first year was 886, including five veterans who entered the program with advanced standing and in 1953, preceding their senior year, became the first Northeastern students to participate in Summer Camp at Fort Belvoir and Fort Gordon.

Adaptation of the work of the ROTC unit to the Northeastern system entailed numerous complex problems. The ten-week Co-operative Plan schedule necessitated adjustment of the units of both military training and related classroom study. The Co-operative Plan also precluded Summer Camp training between the junior and senior years of ROTC students; there were, therefore, few students on campus in their senior year who could pass on to underclass cadets the results of the disciplinary experience of Summer Camp. Academic credit toward the Northeastern degree to be allowed for ROTC class work con-

146

stituted another problem, particularly since different colleges throughout the country have used different bases of evaluation. Here again the ten-week Northeastern semester constituted a special basis for adjustment and correlation of credits; after some experimentation the matter was settled on a permanent basis to the satisfaction of the University and the Army.

Colonel Price served for two years as Commanding Officer of the ROTC unit and then went to an assignment in Europe. During his term of command he established the program, with the necessary adjustments to the special conditions of the Northeastern structure, built up the unit in numbers both of students and instructional personnel, and by the encouragement and sponsorship of activities made ROTC a part of the University rather than a separate and isolated unit.

The University Band was revived to become the ROTC Band, through the use of Army instruments and uniforms and the combination of ROTC and non-ROTC students in the group. The Rifle Team was likewise revived and in following years developed into a group of four teams, with the acceptance by the University of riflery as a minor sport. The MARS (Military Affiliate Radio System) Radio Club made its start in 1951 and later established a co-operative working arrangement with the Northeastern Radio Club.

Also in 1951 a Drill Team was organized. This unit was later chartered as Company E, 8th Regiment of the national ROTC honor society Pershing Rifles. Another group organized in the first year was the Society of American Military Engineers. In 1952–53 a Student Chapter of the Armed Forces Communications and Electronics Association was chartered. It became an active and creative group; in 1956 it assisted in conducting the annual association convention in Boston, in following years sent delegations to the conventions in Washington, and made the first student-produced Northeastern motion picture, a review of ROTC training at the University.

Colonel Price was followed in command of ROTC by Colonel Murray D. Harris, a staff officer during World War II and

147

later. Under his direction the unit expanded in numbers and activities.

A Military Ball was held in 1953, the first of a series of annual events now conducted by the honorary society H. Company, 11th Regiment of the Society of Scabbard and Blade, chartered at Northeastern in 1954. A series of Military News Movies was started to bring to cadets of the underclass groups information and impressions of military ideals and traditions. A program of scholarships, initiated by five University scholarships "in recognition of the constructiveness of the Military Science Program," was extended by scholarships given by Scabbard and Blade and by Pershing Rifles.

As the ROTC unit grew from the original enrollment of 886 to more than 2,800, it became the largest Army ROTC unit in the nation. It distinguished itself not only in size among volunteer undergraduate military units but by the exceptional accomplishments of groups and individuals within the unit. In 1959 the University received a "Certificate of Achievement" from Secretary of the Army William M. Brucker "for outstanding and dedicated service to the United States Army through its highly successful Reserve Officers' Training Corps."

Colonel Harris, PMST for five years at Northeastern, retired in December 1958. His successor, Colonel Sidney S. Davis, was Signal Officer to General Anthony McAuliffe, who, during the Battle of the Bulge, made the famous terse reply "Nuts" to the German demand for surrender. After the war Colonel Davis continued his Army career, and came to Northeastern from his post as Inspector General of the Signal Corps.

XIII

"A FAMILY OF MEN AND WOMEN"

Speaking to the University Corporation during the last year of his Presidency, Dr. Ell said, "Our Northeastern faculty, staff, and students are a family of men and women, boys and girls with deep personal interest in and concern for the hopes and aspirations, the welfare and achievement of every member of the family.

"The radiant spirit, co-operation, and good will which permeate life at Northeastern make the University more than bricks and mortar, more than a place to work or a place to study. It is a place for all—faculty, staff, and students alike—to live with zest, to grow, and to learn.

"I give thanks every day that my life has been cast with associates who are workers, learners, and vibrant spirits—men and women in whom I have always had complete confidence and who have willingly and gladly given themselves, without reserve, to a good cause."

The numerical size of the faculty to which Dr. Ell referred is beyond accurate calculation, in view of the number of people who have worked for Northeastern effectively but briefly and the even larger number who have been part-time teachers or have been associated with the University for special short-term purposes. In other respects than size the family has demonstrated the qualities and changes common to all groups which, though large and diversified, take on homogeneous identity with the passing of time.

149

Origin and Development of Northeastern University

As must always happen through the decades, the attrition of death has left its mark on the Northeastern family. Besides William Lincoln Smith, Winthrop E. Nightingale, and Everett A. Churchill, whose records appear elsewhere in this account of Northeastern, ten men who died while active in the work of the University made substantial contributions and left deep impressions.

The first was William Jefferson Alcott, Jr., a teacher in the Department of Mathematics from 1924 to 1933, when he died from the final effects of injuries incurred in World War I. In the following year members of his family and of the faculty established a fund for the Alcott Award, given annually to a student who has shown outstanding excellence in intellectual achievement beyond that which is required of him in his academic program.

Henry B. Alvord joined the faculty in 1920 and in the next year became Chairman of the Department of Civil Engineering when the placement of students on co-operative work was detached from the department and centered in a new department. He held the chairmanship of Civil Engineering until April of 1939.

Samuel A. S. Strahan was associated with Northeastern from 1912 to 1942. After evening teaching, he was the first new member of the faculty of the School of Co-operative Engineering, appointed in 1917 by Dean Ell. Later he became Chairman of the Department of Chemical Engineering, and in the last four years of his life gave his full time to the teaching of organic chemistry.

Russell Whitney's first work with Northeastern was in the Springfield Division, starting in 1929. In Boston he served for eight years as Dean of the evening School of Business and on the retirement of Galen Light became Comptroller. When he died in 1944, Mr. Whitney left his estate equally to Northeastern and to Dartmouth College, his alma mater.

Two long-time and much-beloved teachers in the Department of Electrical Engineering were Roland G. Porter and

150

"A Family of Men and Women"

Henry E. Richards. Roland Porter, an alumnus of Northeastern, joined the faculty in 1919. He followed Dr. Smith as Chairman of the Department of Electrical Engineering and served for sixteen years until his death in 1953. "Friends of Roland Porter" established a Memorial Fund by which an annual award of books is made to a student of Electrical Engineering who has demonstrated superior campus citizenship. Henry Richards was a teacher of Electrical Engineering from 1921 until his sudden death in 1955. The dedication of the 1950 *Cauldron* said of him: "His positive attitude and honest, forthright efforts made him an example of integrity most highly respected by his classes."

Three other highly respected teachers were taken suddenly from active Northeastern life. Charles F. Barnason was for eleven years member and chairman in the Department of Modern Languages before a fatal heart attack in 1949. R. Lawrence Capon, an accomplished and creative musician as well as an effective and influential teacher of English, was at Northeastern from 1939 until September of 1959. Elmer H. Cutts, Chairman of the Department of History, died suddenly in April of 1960. Dr. Cutts had been at Northeastern since 1941, and had spent the academic year 1958–1959 in India on a Fulbright grant, holding a professorship at Andhra University to design and institute a new graduate program in Pacific history.

Waldemar S. McGuire spent thirty-four years with the Departments of Chemical Engineering and Chemistry. Although the last years of his life were handicapped by increasing illness, he maintained his vigorous interest in teaching and in the development of the Yacht Club, to which he had long been adviser and guiding force. Professor McGuire died in 1958.

Passing decades brought sixteen people of the Northeastern faculty and administration to the age of or the personal need for retirement. The careers of Dr. Speare, Dr. Churchill, and Mr. Light have already been recorded. The other members of the group of sixteen were long-time teachers and staff workers,

151

some of whom "retired" by relinquishing one area of activity and assuming another.

Joseph W. Zeller was Chairman of the Department of Mechanical Engineering from 1921 until 1950, and as Coach of Track in the early years of his association with Northeastern laid foundations on which Edward Parsons and Gerald Tatton developed track to its present status as a major University sport. From 1950 to 1954 Professor Zeller continued to teach courses in the Department of Mechanical Engineering; in following years he contributed his experience and skill to evening teaching in Lincoln Institute.

In 1957 Joseph Spear retired from the Chairmanship of the Department of Mathematics and gave full time to the teaching which he had conducted with such distinction since 1919.

Also in 1957 Harold Melvin retired as Dean of Students but became a full-time member of the Department of English, as he had first been in 1920; he continued to teach the courses in poetry, Shakespeare, and American Literature which have brought satisfaction and rewards to successive generations of Northeastern students.

Robert Bruce, whose association with the University faculty began in 1916 when he became a part-time instructor in the School of Commerce and Finance, retired in the early 1940's but returned to be Acting Dean of the College of Business Administration between the administrations of Asa S. Knowles and Roger S. Hamilton. Thereafter he served the University on special occasions and in his retirement continues to be an active figure in alumni work and a consistent attendant at sports events and social affairs.

Two men identified in the memories of many alumni as close friends and colorful Northeastern personalities were John B. Pugsley and George W. Towle.

John Pugsley became an instructor in mathematics and chemistry in 1918, after having been an Athletic Officer with the A.E.F. He was made Registrar in the following year and in that position supervised the increasingly detailed records of students as a small college grew to be a large university; he also was a teacher of Geology, and did administrative advisory work with veterans of both World War I and World War II. Professor Pugsley retired in 1947 and died in 1953.

George Towle joined the Northeastern faculty in 1923 as one of the early assistants in the Department of Co-operative Work. Second only to Winthrop Nightingale, he was, until his retirement in 1954, the symbol of the Northeastern Co-operative Plan to students and employers during that long period. Professor Towle enjoyed three years of retirement before his death in 1957.

Joseph A. Coolidge retired in 1954 after forty-three years of work with Northeastern, including twenty-three years as Chairman of the Department of Physics. As a major contributor to the informal tradition of the University he identified himself for many years with the Chess Club through his perennial offer to entertain at lunch any student who could defeat him at the game.

Another member of the Department of Physics retired in 1956 after twenty-six years of Northeastern teaching; C. David Johnson, a rocket enthusiast long before rockets became an international preoccupation, moved to Florida for a retirement of leisurely living and part-time teaching.

Albert E. Whittaker was a teacher of Physics and Mechanical Engineering at Northeastern from 1924 until 1956, with a period during which he was on leave and a teacher at M.I.T. He contributed to the early development of student activities, particularly through his work with the Banjo Club, a popular student organization in the 1920's and '30's.

The Department of Drawing was developed by the energy, imagination, and untiring efforts of Eliot F. Tozer, a member of the Northeastern faculty from 1923 to 1958. Following George F. Ashley, who came to Northeastern in 1918 as a brilliant teacher in the pioneer effort to develop departments in the young School of Engineering, Eliot Tozer built the department in size, methods, and equipment; at the same time he made contributions through textbook writing to the field of drawing beyond Northeastern. After leaving the University, Professor Tozer was a technical consultant in drawing equipment and methods of teaching until his death in 1960.

Two women long identified with the daily life of both faculty and students at Northeastern retired in 1957.

Miss Myra White had been a member of the University staff since 1920 and was the first woman member of the faculty. As Librarian, she was a significant figure in the growth of the University and the effort to meet its changing needs.

In another area of growth, Miss Mary B. Foor took over management of the Bookstore in 1918 and at her retirement left a complex business enterprise as a part of the structure and service of the University. Miss Foor, an energetic individualist, was fond of saying that she was the only person who ever "put Dr. Ell out of business"—a correct observation since until her employment books and supplies had been intermittently dispensed by the Dean from a closet near his office.

Miss Edna J. Garrabrant was the first and for some time the only secretary in the Department of Co-operative Work. From 1920 onward, while students were few in number, Miss Garrabrant knew them all and performed a valuable service as unofficial adviser as well as departmental secretary. In 1949 Miss Garrabrant retired to her farm in New Hampshire, and died in 1958.

The stability of the personnel of Northeastern was emphasized in a pleasant and somewhat dramatic way when in 1955 Dr. Ell formed the Twenty-Five-Year Associates, "the full-time members of the Northeastern University faculty and office staff, active and retired, who have given at least twenty-five years of service to the University." The group consisted of forty-six men and women, listed here with the titles which they held in the spring of 1955:

William T. Alexander, Dean of the College of Engineering

Charles O. Baird, Chairman of the Department of Civil Engineering

"A Family of Men and Women"

Chester P. Baker, Chairman of the Department of Chemical Engineering

Mrs. Mabel E. Bean, Administrative Secretary, Buildings and Grounds Department

Robert Bruce, Professor Emeritus of Accounting

Everett A. Churchill, retired Vice President of the University

Laurence F. Cleveland, Associate Professor of Electrical Engineering

Joseph A. Coolidge, Professor Emeritus of Physics

Mrs. Madelyn R. Dowlin, Secretary, Office of the Vice President

Carl S. Ell, President of the University

Albert E. Everett, Director of the Evening Division

Mrs. Daisy M. Everett, Bursar of the University

G. Raymond Fennell, Assistant Director of Admissions

Alfred J. Ferretti, Chairman of the Department of Mechanical Engineering

Mary B. Foor, Manager of the Book Store

Edna J. Garrabrant, Secretary, Department of Co-operative Work

Emil A. Gramstorff, Dean, Graduate Division, College of Engineering

Mrs. Mildred C. Garfield, Administrative Secretary, Office of the Vice President

Charles W. Havice, Dean of Chapel

Frederick W. Holmes, Chairman of the Department of English

Mrs. Bertha Hunter, Telephone Operator

C. David Johnson, Associate Professor of Physics

Wilfred S. Lake, Dean of the College of Liberal Arts

Galen D. Light, retired Secretary of the University

Everett C. Marston, Professor of English

Waldemar S. McGuire, Associate Professor of Chemistry

Harold W. Melvin, Dean of Students

George H. Meserve, Jr., Chairman of the Department of Art

John C. Morgan, Associate Professor of Chemical Engineering

Rudolf O. Oberg, Director of Alumni Relations

Edward S. Parsons, Business Manager of the University

E. Victoria Peterson, Administrative Secretary, Business Office

Mrs. Marjorie G. Prout, Administrative Secretary, Office of the President

Mrs. Mary T. Reynolds, Secretary, Electronics Research Project

Mrs. Jessie P. Rhodes, Secretary to the Director, Department of Student Activities

Milton J. Schlagenhauf, Director of Public Relations

Joseph Spear, Chairman of the Department of Mathematics

Frederick A. Stearns, Professor of Mechanical Engineering

J. Kenneth Stevenson, Superintendent of Buildings and Grounds

Gerald R. Tatton, Head Coach of Track

George W. Towle, Professor Emeritus of Co-operative Work

Eliot F. Tozer, Chairman of the Department of Drawing

Myra White, Librarian

William C. White, Vice President of the University

Joseph W. Zeller, Professor Emeritus of Mechanical Engineering

Saverio Zuffanti, Professor of Chemistry

Since its formation the Twenty-Five-Year Associates have met for an annual spring luncheon as guests of the University and for other social gatherings at the home of Dr. and Mrs. Ell. Each member receives a University chair in Governor Carver design upon becoming a member of the Twenty-Five-Year Associates, and mementoes at later meetings; for example, at one spring luncheon a silver dollar minted in 1898, the year of the founding of the University.

Since the formation of the group three members have been added to the Associates: in 1956 Roger S. Hamilton, Dean of the College of Business Administration and Donald H. Mac-Kenzie, Dean of Lincoln Institute; and in 1958, Rudolph M. Morris, Registrar. No members of the faculty or staff were eligible for membership in 1959 or 1960, since twenty-five years earlier, during the period of depression, Northeastern personnel was not increasing.

Varied reasons explain why so many men and women have spent long spans of time and in many instances their entire working careers at Northeastern.

156

William Crombie White

"A Family of Men and Women"

Some, like Professors Cleveland, Ferretti, Holmes, Meserve, Morgan, Stearns, and Zuffanti, found areas of teaching which gave them complete and permanent satisfaction.

Others found interest and stimulation in different positions as the years passed. Milton J. Schlagenhauf, for example, was a teacher from 1922 to 1926, then Director of Admissions, and beginning in 1952 Director of Public Relations. He was close to the growth and development of the University. G. Raymond Fennell, a Northeastern alumnus of the first class to be graduated from the College of Business Administration, has been a teacher of marketing, business management, economic geography, and economics, and at different times has held the titles Secretary of the Faculty, Assistant Registrar, Executive Assistant to the Vice President, Assistant Director of Admissions, and Adviser to the Student Union.

Throughout the membership of the Twenty-Five-Year Associates the common and unifying reason for length of association with the University clearly is a deep and cumulative concern for the "good cause" which Northeastern represented to them.

The arduous fixed schedules and extra demands on time and energy, the limited facilities, and other restrictions of work at Northeastern in the early years have been alleviated as changes and improvements have become possible.

In 1946 the establishment of the "Permanent Faculty" reinforced the security of teachers and administrators with a retirement plan and a form of tenure. Later benefits, supported by the University or by the University and the worker, have been Blue Cross and Blue Shield supplemented by a Major Medical Plan, Group Insurance, and a Terminal Payment Plan for members of the office staff.

The increasing size of Northeastern and the attendant increase in number and diversity of schools and programs have had conspicuous effects on both teaching faculty and administration.

In recent years teachers have been able to give more time, energy, and talent to research and professional writing, as

159

teaching assignments have been reduced and the total work of the University has spread over a larger group. A further advantage and challenge to the Northeastern teacher has been opportunity for specialization and the direction of advanced study as the graduate programs have developed.

Changes in administrative structure have necessarily involved new positions and specialization of responsibility. In 1925 a simple basic administrative form was adopted; with Dr. Speare as President, Vice President Ell was in charge of the Day Division and Vice President Churchill was in charge of the Evening Division. In contrast, structural changes and additions in the period 1953 to 1959 include the new position of Business Manager, held by Edward S. Parsons; Financial Officer, Lincoln C. Bateson; Provost of the University, William C. White; Dean of the Graduate School, Arthur A. Vernon; Dean of Administration of the Day Colleges, Kenneth G. Ryder; and Dean of Research Administration, Carl F. Muckenhoupt.

The "family of men and women," grown from small numbers to a University total of 900 in the academic year 1959–1960, has been the basis and the source of the vitality, continuity, and progress of Northeastern; it has made possible the history of the University.

XIV

THE GOVERNING BODY

Three different groups—the governing body, the faculty, and the students—are vitally important to the success of a university. From a chronological standpoint the governing body is the first element necessary for the birth and continued existence of a university. The creation of such a group establishes the institution as a legal identity, and this group has the final legal responsibility and control of the actions of the university as a corporate entity. The members of the governing body of a private university are leaders in the community who can bring to the institution their moral and financial support as well as guide it toward worthwhile objectives.

The university administration and faculty and, more particularly, the university president function as the link between the governing body and the students. In America the names of outstanding university professors and outstanding university presidents are generally associated in the mind of the public with our nationally prominent universities. It is quite in keeping with this tradition that the previous chapters in the history of Northeastern have been written largely in terms of the leadership exercised by Northeastern faculty members and administrators.

In the focus of historical perspective, Northeastern University provides an excellent example of the essential contribution of a governing board, a contribution seldom recognized by the

161

public or even by the faculty and students. It is the flexibility of governing boards and their ability to adapt themselves to new situations which account for much of the success of American higher education and, by the same token, of Northeastern University. The Educational Committee and the Board of Directors of the Boston YMCA could hardly have known that they were preparing for Northeastern University when they sponsored the evening law program of 1898. Only through the flexibility of these groups and their response to the success of the first programs was the evolution of Northeastern made possible.

From the early years of the Evening Institute until the incorporation of Northeastern College, controlling authority rested with the Educational Committee, a well established unit in the structure of the Boston YMCA and responsible to the Board of Directors. In 1914–1915 that Committee consisted of William E. Murdock, Albert H. Curtis, and William C. Chick. Separate from the Educational Committee in the same year were the School of Law Corporation, formed in 1904, and the School of Commerce and Finance Corporation, formed in 1911.

The first Trustees of Northeastern College, as announced in the catalog for 1916–1917, were the President of the new college and the twenty Officers and Directors of the Boston YMCA—

> Arthur S. Johnson, President
> Albert H. Curtis, 1st Vice President
> William E. Murdock, 2nd Vice President
> George W. Mehaffey, 3rd Vice President
> George W. Brainard, Secretary
> Lewis A. Crossett, Treasurer

F. W. Carter	J. Grafton Minot
S. B. Carter	W. B. Mossman
William C. Chick	W. H. Newhall
George W. Coleman	Silas Peirce

The Governing Body

Robert G. Dodge

With few changes in personnel this group continued to act as the Board of Trustees of the new college in the years immediately following 1916. An innovation in the personnel of the Board occurred in 1922 when Walton I. Crocker, Robert G. Dodge, and F. R. Carnegie Steele were elected to membership;

163

these three men were the first members, except for the President of Northeastern, who were not at the same time Directors of the Boston YMCA.

A basic change in the structure of the governing body took place in 1936 and 1937 with a revision of the Bylaws of the University and the formation of the Northeastern University Corporation. The background to this change and the details of the meetings which brought about the establishment of the Corporation are recorded in Chapter V; the thinking and planning of that transitional period reflect a fundamental change at that time in the control of Northeastern and the concept of its future. The reorganization gave Northeastern University a governing board composed of leaders in the business, industrial, and cultural community it served. Some of those who had served Northeastern for many years were joined by a large number of other leaders from the broader community; in 1937 the Corporation was composed of seventy-four men.

As planned at its formation, the Corporation meets annually and elects from its membership a Board of Trustees. This board assumes a direct responsibility for governing the University, and is organized into various committees for this purpose. At the present time an Executive Committee and standing committees on Development, Funds and Investments, and Facilities provide an extensive and flexible organization. The Corporation has grown to 130 members and the Board of Trustees to thirty-seven.

From its formation until the present time the Corporation has been of great value to the University, not only as a legally constituted authority but as a body which has provided support and assistance. By personal interest and concern, by monetary gifts, and by influence in the community and throughout New England, members of the Corporation have aided substantially in the construction of the buildings on Huntington Avenue and have contributed both directly and indirectly to the growing stature of Northeastern.

164

The Governing Body

In 1937 the President of the Alumni Association was made a member of the Corporation by virtue of his office. In 1952 the Corporation adopted a plan of Alumni Term Members; by this plan, four alumni are elected each year to the Corporation for four-year terms. In recent years, therefore, the alumni have had a stronger voice in the governing body of their University.

The sustaining support of the Corporation is reflected by the fact that seventeen members of the original group are still members in 1959–1960. They are Arthur A. Ballantine, George L. Barnes, Thomas P. Beal, F. Gregg Bemis, William C. Chick, Paul F. Clark, Albert M. Creighton, Robert G. Dodge, Carl S. Ell, Merrill Griswold, Chandler Hovey, Howard M. Hubbard, Galen D. Light, Edward A. MacMaster, Frank L. Richardson, Leverett Saltonstall, Robert T. P. Storer.

The officers of the Corporation through the years have been as follows—

Chairmen of the Corporation and the Board of Trustees
Robert G. Dodge, 1936–1959
Byron K. Elliott, 1959–

Vice Chairman of the Corporation and the Board of Trustees
Frank L. Richardson, 1936–

Secretary-Treasurer of Northeastern University
Galen D. Light, 1936–1943

Treasurers of the Corporation and the Board of Trustees
Henry N. Andrews, 1943–1946
Robert G. Emerson, 1946–1956
Byron K. Elliott, 1956–1959
Lawrence H. Martin, 1959–

Secretaries of the Corporation and the Board of Trustees
Everett A. Churchill, 1943–1953
Lincoln C. Bateson, 1953–

The standing committees of the Board of Trustees, provided for in the original structure of the Corporation, have made vital contributions to the control, direction, and progress of the University. Of the Executive Committee, for example, Dr. Ell has written, "This Committee has had, and has today, all of the authority of the Board of Trustees in the absence of a meeting of the Board. It is obvious, therefore, that the Execu-

Byron K. Elliott

tive Committee is by far the most powerful committee and actually performs many of the duties in regard to the supervision of the institution which normally would devolve upon the Trustees." The leadership of this and the other standing committees has been continuously in the hands of able men who

166

The Governing Body

maintained a deep interest in Northeastern and contributed significantly to its development. The chronological sequence follows—

Chairmen of the Executive Committee

Edward J. Frost, 1936–1938
Walter Channing, 1938–1954
Frank L. Richardson, 1954–1955
George R. Brown, 1955–1957
David F. Edwards, 1957–1960
S. Bruce Black, 1960–

Chairmen of the Committee on Development

Frank L. Richardson, 1936–1946
Edward Dana, 1946–1960
David F. Edwards, 1960–

Chairmen of the Committee on Funds and Investments

Charles Stetson, 1937–1953
Robert G. Emerson, 1953–1956
Byron K. Elliott, 1956–1959
Lawrence H. Martin, 1959–

Chairmen of the Committee on Facilities

Frederic H. Fay, 1943–1944
Earl P. Stevenson, 1944–

Appendix D in this record of Northeastern is "Northeastern Buildings and Rooms Dedicated to Persons and Created by Individual Gifts." The names of seventeen present and past members of the Corporation appear in this listing—

Godfrey L. Cabot	Edward J. Frost
George H. Clifford	Harry H. Kerr
Robert G. Dodge	Edwin S. Webster, Jr.
Bernard W. Doyle	James L. Richards

Origin and Development of Northeastern University

David F. Edwards   Frank L. Richardson
Carl S. Ell   Joseph G. Riesman
Albert E. Everett   Abbot Stevens
Joseph F. Ford   Robert G. Studley
Edwin S. Webster

In view of the large number of able and distinguished men who have served on the Northeastern University Corporation— for example, fifty-six men were members of the Corporation at the time of their death, from 1937 to 1959—individuals can be cited only on the basis of objective criteria.

Presidents Speare and Ell, Vice President Churchill, and Secretary Galen Light were for many years connecting links between the day-to-day operation and development of the University and its trustees. In the present administration this liaison is carried on by President Knowles and Secretary Lincoln Bateson.

Arthur S. Johnson, member of the Boston YMCA Board of Directors in 1888 and President of the Boston YMCA from 1897 to 1929, was a strong guiding force in the early years of Northeastern history. He was President of the first Board of Trustees of Northeastern College in 1916 and a member of the Corporation from its formation until progressive illness required his retirement from activity in 1949. Among Mr. Johnson's many contributions to the Boston YMCA and to Northeastern was his direction of the fund drive which made possible the construction of the YMCA building on Huntington Avenue.

James L. Richards became associated with Northeastern as a member of the Corporation at its foundation. He made major contributions to Northeastern by stimulating interest in the University among his friends and business associates; by making possible the construction of Richards Hall, the first building on the Huntington Avenue campus; and by continued interest and support until his death in 1955.

Godfrey L. Cabot became a member of the Corporation in 1941. Thereafter, his constant interest in Northeastern, demonstrated by substantial financial contributions and regular at-

168

tendance at Commencements and at special University functions, led to the naming of the Physical Education Center as a tribute to him.

William C. Chick was a member of the Educational Committee of the Boston YMCA in 1915, and a member of the first Board of Trustees of Northeastern College in the following year. Mr. Chick's association with Northeastern has been continuous since that time; he was a charter member of the Corporation and still holds membership in that body.

Robert Gray Dodge, first teacher in the School of Law in 1898, was elected to the Board of Trustees in 1922 and became its Chairman and Chairman of the Executive Committee in 1932. He continued as Chairman of the Corporation and the Board of Trustees from 1936 until 1959, when he retired from active leadership to become Honorary Chairman of the Corporation and the Board of Trustees.

Frank L. Richardson, a graduate of the School of Law, Class of 1909, was the first alumnus to become a Trustee of Northeastern University. Elected in 1930, Mr. Richardson was made Vice Chairman of the Board in 1932; he was the first Vice Chairman of the Corporation and is still serving in that position.

Among the many members of the Corporation who have contributed time, effort, and money to the development of Northeastern buildings, Richard L. Bowditch and Robert Cutler performed a signal service as chairman and vice chairman of the fund-raising campaign for the Library in 1950.

Members of the Corporation have given generously to the general financial support of the University and have created funds for special purposes. Two annual awards which have become increasingly valuable and meaningful to successive generations of students were made possible by Sears B. Condit and Harold D. Hodgkinson.

Mr. Condit, a member of the Corporation from 1936 until his death in 1951, established a student loan fund in 1927, and in 1940 changed it to a permanent fund for monetary awards to juniors and seniors of outstanding scholastic achievement. In

1940 there were eight student recipients; in later years, as the fund was augmented, the number increased to twenty and more annually. The total number of students who have been rewarded, aided, and encouraged by the Sears B. Condit Honor Awards is an impressive continuous group.

Mr. Hodgkinson became a member of the Corporation in 1945. Since 1954 the substantial Harold D. Hodgkinson Achievement Award has been given annually to the student who, in the judgment of a faculty committee, is the most outstanding student from all points of view in the junior class. This award, like the Condit Award, is regarded by the student body as carrying a significance far beyond its monetary value.

The men cited in the preceding paragraphs are representative of the body of business and civic leaders to whom Northeastern has appealed as a vital addition to the educational community of Boston. Without their interest and help, the establishment and development of Northeastern could not have taken place so fruitfully during the first half of the twentieth century.

A complete listing of the Corporation from 1936 onward appears in Appendix B, prepared under the direction of Lincoln C. Bateson, Secretary of the Corporation, and Loring M. Thompson, Director of University Planning.

XV

"A GREAT UNREALIZED
POTENTIAL"

July 1, 1959, was a significant date in the history of Northeastern. On that date the third President of the University took active office.

Preparation for the transfer of leadership was begun in January of 1958, when Dr. Ell announced that he would retire at the end of June, 1959. In a special issue of the *Northeastern News*, he said, "If this institution is to progress, then it should not have its direction suddenly changed. It should go ahead in the same direction. It should be developed and enriched. We must get the right man as the third President."

In May, 1958, the Board of Trustees announced that on unanimous recommendation of a special committee of the Board they had elected as Dr. Ell's successor Asa S. Knowles, then President of the University of Toledo.

Dr. Knowles, a native of Maine and a graduate of Thayer Academy and Bowdoin College, started his professional career at Northeastern in 1931 as a teacher of industrial management, later serving as professor and head of the Department of Industrial Engineering. From 1939 to 1942 he was Dean of the College of Business Administration and Director of the Bureau of Business Research.

Thereafter he was successively Dean of the School of Business Administration and Director of General College Extension at Rhode Island State College, founder and President of the

171

Associated Colleges of Upper New York, Vice President for University Development at Cornell University, and in 1951 President of the University of Toledo.

In 1938 Dr. Knowles was on leave from Northeastern to serve as a member of the secretariat and director of industrial plant tours for the 7th International Management Congress; 1941–1943 he served as Panel Consultant on Training within Industry for the War Manpower Commission; and in 1943–1945 he served as Public Panel member of the New England War Labor Board.

Dr. Knowles held local and national offices in the Society for the Advancement of Management, and in 1938 received the Taylor Key from the Society for service in the field of management. He has received citations from Bergen Junior College (later Fairleigh Dickinson University) and Thayer Academy for distinguished service to higher education, and from the City Council for distinguish service to the City of Toledo, Ohio. In 1938 he was awarded a fellowship in the Institute of Industrial Administration, London, England, for his services in the 7th International Management Congress. In later years he was given honorary membership in the American Institute of Industrial Engineers for contributions to industrial engineering, and in the Engineering Society of Toledo for services to engineering. In 1951 he received an honorary degree from Bowdoin College and in 1957 from Northeastern University.

Various affiliations of the new President, from 1938 to 1960, were Society for the Advancement of Management, American Society of Mechanical Engineers, American Society for Engineering Education, and American Academy of Arts and Sciences; and the honor societies Phi Kappa Pi, Tau Beta Pi, Beta Gamma Sigma, Pi Delta Phi, Blue Key, Sigma Society, Pershing Rifles, and Scabbard and Blade. Current community activities include membership on the Board of Directors of the United Fund of Boston and of the Boston Chamber of Commerce, and on the National Advisory Council, Boston Conference on Distribution.

Asa Smallidge Knowles

Dr. Knowles has written articles on management, industrial engineering, and education for various magazines and journals, and is a contributing editor of *Production Handbook*. He is the author of *Job Evaluation for Hourly and Salaried Workers*, and co-author of *Industrial Management, Management of Manpower,* and *Production Control.*

The third "first lady" of Northeastern is the former Edna Worsnop of Brunswick, Maine; she and Dr. Knowles are the parents of a son, Asa Worsnop, and a daughter, Margaret Anne.

An unusual background to the transfer of leadership at Northeastern was a seven-month period in 1958–1959 during which the President-elect was at the University in an unofficial capacity.

Dr. Knowles reported this experience, under the title "Orientation of a College President," in *The Educational Record* of the American Council on Education. He pointed out that usually the new president of an American college or university assumes his position with little awareness of the major characteristics, concerns, and possibilities of the institution which he is to direct; and, equally important, with an unawareness of the subtleties of the institution. This lack of broad understanding, and deficiency of contact with the thinking, attitudes, and desires of administrators, faculty, students, and alumni often results in a limited perspective by the new president, with resultant errors in judgment and decision. At Northeastern, the period of "orientation" was a planned, cooperative effort to avoid the problems that can arise from abrupt transition of leadership. To Dr. Knowles it was, in his words, a period of "coming home," but coming back to a university which had changed markedly since he had left it in 1942.

At the annual meeting of the University Corporation in May, 1959, Dr. Ell was elected to the position of President Emeritus and Honorary Chancellor of the University. At the same meeting Robert Gray Dodge resigned after twenty-three years as Chairman of the Corporation and twenty-seven years as Chairman of the Board of Trustees, and was elected Honorary Chairman of the Corporation. He was succeeded as Chairman of the Corporation and the Board of Trustees by Byron K. Elliott, Treasurer of the Corporation and the Board of Trustees and President of the John Hancock Mutual Life Insurance Company. Lawrence H. Martin, Executive Vice President, The National Shawmut Bank of Boston, was elected to succeed Judge Elliott as Treasurer of the Corporation and the Board of Trustees.

At the Faculty Inaugural Dinner on September 8, 1959, President Knowles, speaking on *A Look Ahead*, concluded with a summary of his views of the future of Northeastern—

"At this time we can forecast the following:

"We shall cling to our present aims and objectives as now defined—Co-operative education, adult education, and special service education for industry.

"We shall strive to consolidate and strengthen the gains and growths accomplished already. This requires that we strive constantly to improve our efficiency, organization, and staff.

"We shall strive to improve the quality of our student body and graduates by improving our selection of students and enhancing the quality of instruction. Thereby we shall serve better the community and nation.

"We shall make additions to our programs and services only as they conform to established objectives and can be operated on a sound financial basis.

"We shall give priority in fund raising to augmenting our endowments and funds to support the programs and services now provided by the University.

"We shall keep a proper balance in the instructional and research activities of our faculty.

"We shall continue to operate this University on a sound financial basis, doing only those things that we can afford to do and expanding as we have resources available. In brief, we shall operate in the black.

"If we adhere to these principles as we operate from day to

176

day and make plans for the future, we can move forward with confidence. . . . Northeastern University has a great unrealized potential; let us work together to realize it."

The implementation of the principles, attitudes, and objectives stated and implied in Dr. Knowles' inaugural address took shape and became increasingly evident as the academic year 1959–1960 progressed.

A significant change in administrative organization was effected by the creation of three new positions and the appointment of staff members to fill them—Assistant to the President, John S. Bailey (later appointed to the position of Director of Public Relations); Director of the Office of University Planning, Loring M. Thompson; Director of the Office of University Development, F. Weston Prior.

A change in the structure of the University was the establishment of a fifth college, announced in February of 1960 and to become effective in July of that year. University College, supplementing and reinforcing the Colleges of Engineering, Business Administration, Liberal Arts, and Education, is designed to provide improved status for the growing number of part-time students and programs in evening education leading to associate and bachelor degrees. It will develop courses and curricula related to the subject matter offered in the other Northeastern colleges, but adapted to the needs and interests of employed people who wish to undertake or complete a program of higher education during evening hours.

Simultaneously with the establishment of University College, the evening School of Business was merged with the College of Business Administration, completing a fusion of day and evening programs of instruction which was already in effect in engineering, liberal arts, and education.

In future years these structural changes will become increasingly significant. The bachelor's degree will be earned at Northeastern by day study, evening study, or a combination of day and evening work. With the same college admission requirements applying to all curricula in Engineering, Business Administration, Liberal Arts, and Education, and with the same quantitative and qualitative standards applied to programs in the four colleges, different degrees in the same or similar fields will in future be eliminated, and the Northeastern degree will have the same value and significance whether earned by day or evening study.

Also in 1960 an Office of Adult and Continuing Education was established, to develop and promote all evening programs and to offer special educational services as they may be requested or foreseen. Divisions within this Office are the well established Bureau of Business and Industrial Training, and a Department of Special Services.

The development of the new University College and the Office of Adult and Continuing Education is under the direction of Albert E. Everett. Dr. Everett has been associated with Northeastern since 1927; in 1945 he became Dean of the School of Business and Director of the Evening Division.

Other academic changes in 1959–1960 were an extension of graduate study in engineering and the establishment of an evening undergraduate program in engineering.

A master's program in Electrical Engineering was first offered in 1956, and extended to Civil and Mechanical Engineering in the following year. This work was a combination of day and evening classes. Beginning in the fall of 1960, these curricula, with the addition of Chemical Engineering, were administered on a uniform Co-operative Work schedule of ten-week alternating periods of day classes and engineering practice.

An innovation in engineering study in New England was the undergraduate program in Electrical Engineering, beginning in the fall of 1960, to be conducted in the evening over a nine-year period, and made up of the same courses and with the same requirements as those of the day curriculum.

The increasing complexity of Northeastern resulted in added delegation of responsibility to faculty members and faculty committees during 1959–1960. In each of the colleges

178

a Curriculum Committee was formed, to analyze current curricula and to evaluate new courses and proposed changes. The University Committee on Faculty Policy was reconstituted on the basis of membership by election of representatives of the teaching faculties of the colleges, with a chairman elected by the Committee from its membership.

The structure and objectives of these two committees were the result of administrative recommendation. On the initiative of the faculty, in 1960, a Northeastern Chapter of the American Association of University Professors was established.

A major addition to the property of the University was the purchase of the Boston Storage Warehouse, announced in July, 1959. Like the adjoining property on Huntington Avenue where the Boston Opera House formerly stood, the Warehouse acquisition was of primary importance in adding nearly 60,000 square feet of land to the Northeastern campus. The building, made up of ten units constructed at different times during the first quarter of the century, contains floor space over four times that of Richards Hall. During 1959–1960 studies were carried on to determine whether the Warehouse should be remodeled for educational purposes, or demolished to make room for new construction.

On April 21, 1960, another of the anniversaries in Northeastern's history took place. An afternoon convocation and an evening dinner celebrated the fiftieth year of the College of Engineering and of Co-operative Education at the University. A special issue of the *Northeastern News*, edited by Charles Fuller '60, reviewed the history of co-operative education at Northeastern and in the United States. At the dinner, Dr. John L. Burns '30, President, Radio Corporation of America, was the speaker. Dr. Burns, one of Northeastern's most distinguished alumni, received his undergraduate education in the College of Engineering, under the Co-operative Plan.

At the convocation and at the dinner, President Knowles made citations to the following—

179

Origin and Development of Northeastern University

Carl Stephens Ell, ". . . whose leadership throughout half a century inspired courage and fidelity in his colleagues and helped them build an ever finer institution of learning."

John R. Leighton '14, "A member of the pioneer group of 'co-ops,' whose dedicated service as a teacher in the evening programs of Lincoln Institute extends over nearly half a century."

Twenty members of the faculty and administration who had spent thirty-three years or more in the service of Northeastern and its development—

William T. Alexander, Dean of the College of Engineering
Charles O. Baird, Professor of Civil Engineering
Chester P. Baker, Professor of Chemical Engineering
Robert Bruce, Professor Emeritus of Accounting
Joseph A. Coolidge, Professor Emeritus of Physics
Albert E. Everett, Dean of the School of Business and Director of the Evening Division
Alfred J. Ferretti, Professor of Mechanical Engineering
Emil A. Gramstorff, Dean of Graduate Engineering Programs
Charles W. Havice, Professor of Sociology and Dean of Chapel
Frederick W. Holmes, Professor of English
Wilfred S. Lake, Dean of the College of Liberal Arts
Everett C. Marston, Professor of English
Harold W. Melvin, Professor of English and former Dean of Students
George H. Meserve, Professor of Art
Edward S. Parsons, Business Manager of the University
Milton J. Schlagenhauf, Co-ordinator of Functions
Joseph Spear, Professor of Mathematics
Frederick A. Stearns, Professor of Mechanical Engineering
William C. White, Vice President and Provost of the University

"A Great Unrealized Potential"

Joseph W. Zeller, Professor Emeritus of Mechanical Engineering

Three fifty-year co-operating companies—

Boston Edison Company
Boston Gas Company
Wm. S. Crocker, Inc.

Twenty alumni of the College of Engineering, "for distinguished attainment"—

Donald A. Bean '35, Assistant Director of Product Standards, Campbell Soup Company

Maurice H. Bigelow '24, Vice President, Research and Engineering, Allied Chemical Corporation

Richard B. Brown, Jr. '22, Division Head, Commercial Lighting Sales, Boston Edison Company

Henry F. Callahan '26, Vice President and General Manager, Sylvania Lighting Products

Elmer T. Carlson '25, Executive Vice President, Electric Distribution Products, Inc.

William S. Chapin '27, Project Engineering, St. Lawrence Seaway Power Authority of the State of New York

James N. DeSerio '35, Consulting Engineer

Ivan G. Easton '38, Vice President for Engineering, General Radio Company

Howard T. Engstrom '22, Vice President and Director of Marketing, Remington Rand Univac Division of Sperry Rand Corporation

Calvin A. King '44, President, Bird Machine Company

Edward B. Landry '28, Director of Safety and Health, United States Post Office Department

Alfred E. Lonnberg '32, Vice President of Sanborn Company

Robert E. Madsen '31, Marine Sales Manager, Mobil International Oil Company

Joseph P. McGuckian '30, Vice President, William S. Libbey Company

Charles W. Perry '34, Assistant Manager, Matchieson Company

Leon P. Sudrabian '36, Consulting Engineer, Electro Rust Proofing Corporation

Harold A. Swanson '30, Vice President, E. F. Drew & Co., Inc.

Eugene J. Vogel '36, Treasurer, Wes Julian Construction Company

Roger G. Witherell '27, Officer in charge of Seabee Reserve Training for the U. S. Navy

Alfred K. Wright '31, Vice President, Operations, Tung-Sol Electric, Inc.

The changes and innovations which took place at Northeastern in 1959–1960 are forecasts of the future of the University. The details of that future are impossible of prediction, but outlines of the future are apparent.

It is evident that Northeastern will grow in stature as it adapts itself to a changing world. A Committee on Planning, made up of members of the faculty and administration, recommended in 1960 that during the period until 1970 undergraduate education at Northeastern should grow less rapidly than during the period from 1920 to 1960, and that graduate education should increase substantially.

The reasons for these recommendations rise from basic changes seen by the Committee as taking place in higher education in Massachusetts as well as in the nation. With the inevitable development of public-supported regional colleges, state and community, and the establishment of new private colleges in different sections of the Commonwealth, the commuting undergraduate population of the future will be spread over a wide area rather than being concentrated in the Boston colleges. With the increasing importance of advanced degrees and specialized training, in the humanities as well as in technical and scientific fields, the need for broadened and intensified opportunities in graduate study will develop.

In view of these two trends, Northeastern's contribution to the future may well be a stabilizing of its undergraduate work, with progressive higher standards through selectivity of students; and an extension of graduate work.

This development would necessarily correlate with further expansion and acceleration of research. It would require extensive and specialized personnel, housing, equipment, and library facilities. Moreover, coupled with the fulfillment of University College and the Office of Adult and Continuing Education, graduate study and research would project into the future the Northeastern tradition of flexibility and adaptation as means toward community and national service—a tradition which had its origin in the Evening Institute for Young Men of the Boston YMCA.

Any educational institution which endures must change with changing times. Each new period requires different leadership, personnel, and methods, if the direction and the potential of the period are to be seen, understood, and realized. With due allowance for the limited perspective which immediacy of time imposes, the pattern of the history of Northeastern can be viewed in three broad periods. The central figure in each period is not only a symbol but a determining force.

Dr. Speare provided the idealism, optimism, and adventuresome spirit needed in his time to lay foundations and chart directions by experimentation and by trial and error.

Dr. Ell built upon the foundations and broadened the scope of earlier directions, to establish Northeastern University as a physical entity and a recognized university.

The third President, Dr. Knowles, with some talents and concepts similar to those of his predecessors but with special qualities now needed in his own time, will determine the future.

APPENDIX A

NORTHEASTERN UNIVERSITY CHRONOLOGY

1896—Evening Institute of the Boston YMCA established

1897—Special courses in Law, Elementary Electricity, Advanced Electricity, by the Lowell Institute, under the auspices of the Evening Institute of the Boston YMCA

1898—Department of Law of the Evening Institute established

1902—First graduating class (21) from the School of Law

1903—Automobile School of the Evening Institute established

1904—School of Law incorporated, with power to grant the LL. B. degree
Evening Polytechnic School (Lincoln Institute) established

1907—School of Commerce and Finance (School of Business) established

1909—Day co-operative education in engineering started
Day Preparatory School (The Huntington School) established

1911—School of Commerce and Finance incorporated, with degree-granting power
Botolph Building occupied

1913—Huntington Avenue Building of the Boston YMCA occupied

1916—Northeastern College of the Boston Young Men's Christian Association incorporated, March 30
Student newspaper *The Co-op* started

1917–Frank Palmer Speare inaugurated as first President, March 30

1920–Northeastern College authorized to grant degrees of B.C.E., B.M.E., B.E.E., B. Ch. E.

1921–The Senate, honor society of the School of Engineering, organized

1922–Northeastern College renamed Northeastern University School of Business Administration established

1923–Degree-granting power extended, with exceptions of medical and dental degrees, A.B., and B.S.

1925–Sigma Society, honor society of the College of Business Administration, organized

1926–Automobile School closed

King Husky I, University mascot, crowned, March 9

1929–First purchase of land on Huntington Avenue

First year of hockey as a varsity sport

1930–Degree-granting power extended to include B.S. with specifications

Acquisition of Botolph Building from the Boston YMCA

Acquisition of Huntington Field in Brookline

1933–First season of football as a varsity sport

1935–College of Liberal Arts established

Degree-granting power extended, with exception of medical and dental degrees

College of Engineering accredited by the University of the State of New York

1936–Northeastern University Corporation established

1937–The Academy, honor society of the College of Liberal Arts, organized

1938–Richards Hall occupied

1939–Curricula in Civil, Mechanical, Electrical, and Industrial Engineering accredited by the Engineers' Council for Professional Development

1940–Carl Stephens Ell inaugurated as second President, November 19

University added to the list of institutional members of

the New England Association of Colleges and Secondary Schools

First Northeastern University teaching fellows (Department of Chemistry)

1941—College of Business Administration and College of Liberal Arts accredited by the University of the State of New York

Department of Chemistry accredited by the American Chemical Society

University made an institutional member of the American Council on Education

Chapter of Tau Beta Pi, national honor society, established in the College of Engineering

Science Hall occupied

1942—University made an institutional member of the Association of American Colleges

Curriculum in Chemical Engineering accredited by the Engineers' Council for Professional Development

1943—Women students admitted to the Day Colleges

School of Law accredited by the University of the State of New York

1945—School of Law made a member of the Association of American Law Schools

1947—Student Center occupied

1948—Fiftieth Anniversary convocation and banquet, October 2

1950—Transfer of The Huntington School to the Boston YMCA

Evening graduate programs in the College of Engineering started

1951—Army R.O.T.C. unit established

1952—Library Building occupied

1953—College of Education established

Closing of School of Law announced

1954—Physical Education Center occupied

Faculty Committee on Development and Co-ordination of Research formed

1956—Hayden Hall occupied

1957—Physical Education Center named Godfrey Lowell Cabot Physical Education Center

1958—Student Center Building named Carl Stephens Ell Student Center

Graduate School established

1959—Graduate Center occupied

Library Building named Robert Gray Dodge Library

Asa Smallidge Knowles inaugurated as third President, September 8

1960—University College established

Celebration of 50th year of the College of Engineering and of Co-operative Education at Northeastern, April 21

APPENDIX B

MEMBERS OF THE CORPORATION
1936-1960

Members of the Corporation—The regular members of the Corporation are elected for an indefinite period.

Alumni Term Members of the Corporation—Each year four alumni are elected to the Corporation for a four-year term. Those elected once are not eligible for re-election as Alumni Term Members.

Term Members of the Corporation—Alumni association presidents are *ex officio* term members of the Corporation during their period of office as president.

Members of the Board of Trustees—Each year ten members of the Corporation are elected for four-year terms on the Board of Trustees. Members are eligible for re-election at any time.

Standing Committees—Members of the Board of Trustees are eligible for appointment to the standing committees of the Board. These are the Executive Committee, the Committee on Development, the Committee on Facilities, and the Committee on Funds and Investments.

Abbott, Joseph Florence, *formerly Chairman of the Board, American Sugar Refining Company.* Member of the Corporation, 1941–54.

Abrams, Julius, *President, Poley-Abrams Corporation.* Alumni Term Member, 1960– .

189

Adams, Charles Francis [Sr.], *formerly Chairman of the Board, State Street Trust Company.* Member of the Corporation, 1936–53; Board of Trustees, 1937–44. (Deceased)

Adams, Charles Francis [Jr.], *Chairman of the Board, Raytheon Company.* Member of the Corporation, 1953– .

Adams, Wilman Edward, *formerly General Secretary, Boston Young Men's Christian Association.* Member of the Corporation, 1936–46; Board of Trustees, 1936–46. (Deceased)

Allen, Asa Samuel, *Attorney at Law: Willard, Allen & Mulkern.* Term Member of the Corporation, 1946–49.

Amory, Roger, *formerly Chairman of the Board, Rockland-Atlas National Bank of Boston.* Member of the Corporation, 1936–51. (Deceased)

Anderson, O. Kelley, *President and Director, New England Mutual Life Insurance Company.* Member of the Corporation, 1945– .

Andrews, Henry Nathaniel, *formerly Vice President, Old Colony Trust Company.* Member of the Corporation, 1940–60; Board of Trustees, 1941–46; Executive Committee, 1943–46; Committee on Development, 1943–46; Treasurer of the Corporation and the Board of Trustees, 1943–46. (Deceased)

Avila, Charles F., *President, Boston Edison Company.* Member of the Corporation, 1960– .

Ayer, Frederick, *Trustee and Director.* Member of the Corporation, 1946– .

Babst, Earl D., *Chairman of the Board, American Sugar Refining Company.* Member of the Corporation, 1936–40.

Baker, George Bramwell, *formerly Banker and Trustee.* Member of the Corporation, 1936–37. (Deceased)

Baldwin, Robert, *Vice President, Museum of Fine Arts, Boston; formerly Senior Vice President, Second National Bank of Boston.* Member of the Corporation, 1937–44.

190

Appendix B

Ballantine, Arthur Atwood, *formerly Attorney at Law, Dewey, Ballantine, Bushby, Palmer & Wood.* Member of the Corporation, 1936-60; Board of Trustees, 1936-45; Committee on Development, 1936-43. (Deceased)

Barnes, George Louis, *Vice President and Director, Heywood-Wakefield Company.* Member of the Corporation, 1936- ; Board of Trustees, 1936- ; Executive Committee, 1936-56; Committee on Facilities, 1956- .

Bateson, Lincoln Carr, *Financial Officer, Northeastern University.* Secretary of the Corporation and the Board of Trustees, 1953- ; Member of the Corporation, 1959- ; Board of Trustees, 1959- ; Committee on Funds and Investments, 1959- .

Beal, Thomas Prince, *Chairman, Directors Advisory Board, State Street Bank and Trust Company.* Member of the Corporation, 1936- .

Bemis, Farwell Gregg, *Chairman, Bemis Bro. Bag Company.* Member of the Corporation, 1936- ; Board of Trustees, 1939- ; Executive Committee, 1943-51; Committee on Development, 1951- .

Bigelow, Edward Livingston, *Chairman of the Board, State Street Bank and Trust Company.* Member of the Corporation, 1959- .

Black, S. Bruce, *Chairman of the Board, Liberty Mutual Insurance Companies.* Member of the Corporation, 1942- ; Board of Trustees, 1956- ; Committee on Facilities, 1956-58; Executive Committee, 1958- , Chairman, 1960- .

Blackwell, Lawrence Franklin, *Vice President and Director, Pneumatic Scale Corporation, Ltd.* Alumni Term Member of the Corporation, 1959- .

Blanchard, Raymond H., *President, B. F. Goodrich-Hood Rubber Company; Chairman of the Board of Directors, First National Bank of Malden.* Member of the Corporation, 1956- .

Bloch, William Albert, *Comptroller, Cabot Corporation.* Alumni Term Member of the Corporation, 1955-59.

191

Bottomly, John S., *Attorney at Law.* Member of the Corporation, 1951–54.

Bowditch, Richard Lyon, *formerly Chairman of the Board, C. H. Sprague & Son Company.* Member of the Corporation, 1948–59; Board of Trustees, 1950–59; Committee on Development, 1950–59. (Deceased)

Bradford, Cecil Babcock, *President, Lewis E. Tracy Company.* Alumni Term Member of the Corporation, 1955–59.

Bradlee, Henry Goddard, *formerly Vice President, Stone & Webster, Inc.* Member of the Corporation, 1940–47; Board of Trustees, 1941–47; Committee on Funds and Investments, 1941–47; Committee on Development, 1943–47. (Deceased)

Bradley, Samuel Whitney, *Vice President, Eaton & Howard, Inc.* Alumni Term Member of the Corporation, 1960– .

Brask, Henry, *President, Brask Engineering Company.* Alumni Term Member of the Corporation, 1957– .

Brown, George Russell, *Chairman of the Board, United Shoe Machinery Corporation.* Member of the Corporation, 1949– ; Board of Trustees, 1955– ; Committee on Facilities, 1952–54; Executive Committee, 1954– , Chairman, 1955–57.

Brown, Martin, *President, J. & M. Brown Company, Inc.* Alumni Term Member of the Corporation, 1959– .

Bruce, Robert, *Professor Emeritus of Accounting, Northeastern University.* Term Member of the Corporation, 1946–48. (Deceased)

Burke, George Leo, *Consulting Engineer.* Alumni Term Member of the Corporation, 1959– .

Burnham, George A., *formerly Consulting Engineer, Allis-Chalmers Manufacturing Company.* Member of the Corporation, 1941–61. (Deceased)

Burns, John L., *President, Radio Corporation of America.* Member of the Corporation, 1957– ; Board of Trustees, 1960– ; Committee on Development, 1960– .

Appendix B

Burt, Ashley D., *Assistant Treasurer, Waldorf System, Inc.* Term Member of the Corporation, 1957–59.

Cabot, Godfrey Lowell, *Honorary Chairman of the Board, Cabot Corporation.* Member of the Corporation, 1941– ; Board of Trustees, 1942– ; Committee on Development, 1943– .

Cabot, Louis Wellington, *President, Cabot Corporation.* Member of the Corporation, 1953– ; Board of Trustees, 1954– ; Committee on Facilities, 1955–56; Executive Committee, 1956– .

Cabot, Paul Codman, *Chairman of the Board, State Street Investment Corporation.* Member of the Corporation, 1936–48; Board of Trustees, 1944–48; Committee on Development, 1945–48.

Carey, Charles C., *President, General Radio Company.* Member of the Corporation, 1958– ; Board of Trustees, 1960– ; Committee on Facilities, 1960– .

Carlson, Elmer T., *President, The Trumbull Electric Manufacturing Company.* Member of the Corporation, 1947–55.

Carpenter, Frank Pierce, *formerly President, Amoskeag Paper Mills.* Member of the Corporation, 1936–38. (Deceased)

Carter, Winthrop Lakey, *formerly President, Nashua Gummed and Coated Paper Company.* Member of the Corporation, 1939–44. (Deceased)

Caverly, Gardner Arthur, *Executive Vice President, The New England Council.* Alumni Term Member of the Corporation, 1957– .

Channing, Walter, *formerly President, Walter Channing, Inc.* Member of the Corporation, 1937–54; Board of Trustees, 1937–54; Committee on Development, 1937–43; Executive Committee, 1938–54, Chairman, 1938–54. (Deceased)

Chapman, Richard P., *President, New England Merchants National Bank of Boston.* Member of the Corporation, 1956– .

Chase, Theodore, *Partner, Palmer, Dodge, Gardner & Bradford.* Member of the Corporation, 1956– .

Cherry, Robert William, *Market Administrator, Federal Milk Market Agency.* Term Member of the Corporation, 1950–51.

Chick, William Converse, *Chairman of the Board, John H. Pray & Sons Company.* Member of the Corporation, 1936– ; Board of Trustees, 1936– ; Committee on Funds and Investments, 1936–41; Executive Committee, 1941– .

Ching, Cyrus Stuart, *Consultant, Labor-Management Relations.* Member of the Corporation, 1946–51.

Choate, Robert Burnett, *Publisher and President, Boston Herald-Traveler Corporation.* Member of the Corporation, 1948–57.

Churchill, Everett Avery, *formerly Vice President, Northeastern University.* Member of the Corporation, 1936–59; Board of Trustees, 1941–52; Committee on Development, 1939–41, Chairman, 1939–41; Secretary of the Corporation and the Board of Trustees, 1943–52. (Deceased)

Clark, Paul Foster, *Chairman of the Board, John Hancock Mutual Life Insurance Company.* Member of the Corporation, 1936– ; Board of Trustees, 1936–55; Committee on Development, 1936–43, 1945–55.

Clifford, George Henry, *formerly President, Stone & Webster Service Corporation.* Member of the Corporation, 1948–52. (Deceased)

Collins, William Hazel, *formerly Vice President, Shipbuilding Division, Bethlehem Steel Company.* Member of the Corporation, 1944–48. (Deceased)

Condit, Sears B., *formerly Chairman of the Board, The Chase-Shawmut Company.* Member of the Corporation, 1936–51. (Deceased)

Connolly, T. Paul, *Vice President and General Manager, Thermo-Fax Sales, Inc.* Term Member of the Corporation, 1960– .

Cookingham, Howard C., *Vice President, D. H. Litter Company, Inc.* Term Member of the Corporation, 1949–51; Alumni Term Member of the Corporation, 1958– .

Coolidge, Amory, *Executive Vice President, Pepperell Manufacturing Company.* Member of the Corporation, 1945–59.

Coolidge, William Appleton, *Chairman of the Board, National Research Corporation.* Member of the Corporation, 1960– .

Cottle, George T., *formerly Treasurer, Charles E. Crofoot Gear Corporation.* Member of the Corporation, 1952–58; Board of Trustees, 1954–58; Committee on Development, 1954–58. (Deceased)

Creighton, Albert Morton, *Trustee and Director.* Member of the Corporation, 1936– .

Crocker, Paul Earl, *Treasurer and Secretary, Pepperell Manufacturing Company.* Alumni Term Member of the Corporation, 1952–56.

Crockett, Elton Guild, *President, Crockett Mortgage Company.* Alumni Term Member of the Corporation, 1954–58; Member of the Corporation, 1959– ; Board of Trustees, 1960– ; Committee on Development, 1960– .

Curtis, Edgar Hazen, *formerly with Charles F. Baker Company.* Member of the Corporation, 1937. (Deceased)

Cutler, Robert, *United States Executive Director, Inter-American Development Bank; Special Assistant to the Secretary of the Treasury.* Member of the Corporation, 1946– .

Dalton, Marshall Bertrand, *Chairman of the Boards, Boston Manufacturers Mutual and Mutual Boiler & Machinery Insurance Companies.* Member of the Corporation, 1945– ; Board of Trustees, 1947–54; Committee on Funds and Investments, 1947–54.

Damon, Roger Conant, *President and Chairman of the Executive Committee, The First National Bank of Boston.* Member of the Corporation, 1960– .

Dana, Edward, *Transit Consultant; formerly General Manager,*

Metropolitan Transit Authority. Member of the Corporation, 1942– ; Board of Trustees, 1945– ; Committee on Development, 1945–60, Chairman, 1946–60; Executive Committee, 1946– ; Committee on Facilities, 1960– .

Dane, Edward, *President, Brookline Trust Company.* Member of the Corporation, 1942– .

Dane, Ernest Blaney, *formerly President, Brookline Trust Company.* Member of the Corporation, 1939–42. (Deceased)

Daniels, James William, *The Daniels Agency.* Term Member of the Corporation, 1943–45.

Darrin, Ralph Mead, *Commercial Vice President, General Electric Company.* Member of the Corporation, 1949–54.

Dart, Justin Whitlock, *President, Rexall Drug Company.* Member of the Corporation, 1944–48.

Davidson, William J., Trustee and Director. Member of the Corporation, 1936–47; Board of Trustees, 1936–44.

Davis, Nathanael Vining, *President, Aluminium, Ltd.* Member of the Corporation, 1957–61.

Dean, James, *formerly Chairman of the Executive Committee, Boston Safe Deposit and Trust Company.* Member of the Corporation, 1936–42. (Deceased)

Dennett, Carl Pullen, *formerly Trustee and Director.* Member of the Corporation, 1947–55. (Deceased)

Dennison, Henry Sturgis, *President, Dennison Manufacturing Company.* Member of the Corporation, 1936–40.

Dignan, Thomas G., *formerly President and General Manager, Boston Edison Company.* Member of the Corporation, 1954–60. (Deceased)

Dillon, Frederick Joseph, *Judge of Probate, Suffolk County, Massachusetts.* Term Member of the Corporation, 1949–54.

Dodge, Robert Gray, *Attorney at Law, Palmer, Dodge, Gardner & Bradford.* Member of the Corporation, 1936– ; Board of Trustees, 1936– ; Chairman of the Corporation and the

Board of Trustees, 1936–59; Executive Committee, 1959– ; Honorary Chairman of the Corporation and the Board of Trustees, 1959– .

Doyle, Bernard W., *formerly Vice President, Du Pont Viscoloid Company.* Member of the Corporation, 1944–49. (Deceased)

Draper, Paul Augustus, *Chairman of the Board, Draper & Company, Inc.* Member of the Corporation, 1936–48.

Eaton, Charles F., *President, The Clement Manufacturing Company.* Member of the Corporation, 1936–44; Board of Trustees, 1936–37.

Edwards, David Frank, *Honorary Chairman of the Board, Saco-Lowell Shops.* Member of the Corporation, 1943– ; Board of Trustees, 1944– ; Committee on Development, 1945–54, 1960– , Chairman, 1960– ; Executive Committee, 1954– , Chairman, 1957–60.

Ell, Carl Stephens, *President Emeritus and Honorary Chancellor, Northeastern University.* Member of the Corporation, 1936– ; Board of Trustees, 1940– ; Executive Committee, 1959– .

Elliott, Byron Kauffman, *President, John Hancock Mutual Life Insurance Company.* Member of the Corporation, 1954– ; Board of Trustees, 1955– ; Committee on Facilities, 1955–56; Treasurer of the Corporation and the Board of Trustees, 1956–59; Executive Committee, 1956–59; Committee on Funds and Investments, 1956–59, Chairman, 1956–59; Chairman of the Corporation and the Board of Trustees, 1959– .

Ellison, William Partridge, *Vice President, Proctor Ellison Company.* Member of the Corporation, 1941– ; Board of Trustees, 1944– ; Committee on Development, 1945– .

Ellms, Lindsay, *District Manager, Ohio Brass Company.* Term Member of the Corporation, 1939–41.

Ely, Joseph Buell, *formerly Governor, Commonwealth of Massachusetts.* Member of the Corporation, 1937–46. (Deceased)

Emerson, Robert Greenough, *Trustee; formerly Senior Vice President, The First National Bank of Boston.* Member of the Corporation, 1944– ; Board of Trustees, 1946– ; Executive Committee, 1946– ; Treasurer of the Corporation and the Board of Trustees, 1946–56; Committee on Funds and Investments, 1952–56, Chairman, 1953–56; Committee on Facilities, 1956–58.

Erickson, Joseph Austin, *President, The New England Council.* Member of the Corporation, 1953– .

Erickson, Robert, *Executive Vice President, Beckman Instruments, Inc.* Alumni Term Member of the Corporation, 1957– ; Board of Trustees, 1960– ; Committee on Development, 1960– .

Everett, Albert Ellsworth, *Dean of Continuing Education, Northeastern University.* Alumni Term Member of the Corporation, 1952–56.

Falvey, Timothy James, *formerly President, Massachusetts Bonding & Insurance Company.* Member of the Corporation, 1936–39. (Deceased)

Falvey, Wallace, *formerly President, Massachusetts Bonding & Insurance Company.* Member of the Corporation, 1948–58. (Deceased)

Farley, John Wells, *formerly Attorney at Law, Herrick, Smith, Donald, Farley & Ketchum.* Member of the Corporation, 1940–59; Board of Trustees, 1941–59; Committee on Development, 1945–59. (Deceased)

Farwell, Frank L., *Vice President, Liberty Mutual Insurance Company.* Member of the Corporation, 1956– ; Board of Trustees, 1958– ; Committee on Funds and Investments, 1958– .

Fay, Frederic Harold, *formerly Consulting Engineer, Fay, Spofford & Thorndike, Inc.* Member of the Corporation, 1936–44; Board of Trustees, 1936–44; Executive Committee, 1936–44; Committee on Development, 1936–37;

Appendix B

Committee on Facilities, 1943–44, Chairman, 1943–44. (Deceased)

Flood, Frank Lee, *formerly Partner, Metcalf & Eddy.* Alumni Term Member of the Corporation, 1952–56; Member of the Corporation, 1957–58. (Deceased)

Forbes, Allan, *Chairman of the Board, State Street Trust Company.* Member of the Corporation, 1936–45.

Ford, Joseph Fabian, *President, Ford Manufacturing, Inc.* Member of the Corporation, 1945– .

Foss, Noble, *President, Maverick Mills.* Member of the Corporation, 1949– .

Freeman, Ernest Bigelow, *formerly President, B. F. Sturtevant Company.* Member of the Corporation, 1942–58; Board of Trustees, 1944–58; Committee on Development, 1945–51; Executive Committee, 1951–58. (Deceased)

Frost, Edward J., *formerly President, Wm. Filene's Sons Company.* Member of the Corporation, 1936–44; Board of Trustees, 1936–44; Executive Committee, 1936–40, Chairman, 1936–38; Committee on Development, 1936–40. (Deceased)

Ganse, Franklin Wile, *formerly with Ganse-King Estate Service.* Member of the Corporation, 1936–47. (Deceased)

Gardner, George Peabody, *Trustee and Director.* Member of the Corporation, 1936–40.

Garth, William Willis, Jr., *President, Compugraphic Corporation.* Member of the Corporation, 1955– .

Gibson, Harvey Dow, *Trustee and Director.* Member of the Corporation, 1936–46; Board of Trustees, 1936–45.

Gill, John Joseph, *President, John J. Gill Associates, Inc.* Term Member of the Corporation, 1958–59.

Gow, Charles Rice, *formerly Chairman of the Board, Warren Brothers Company.* Member of the Corporation, 1936–37. (Deceased)

199

Grandin, John Livingston, Jr., *Secretary, The Gillette Company.* Member of the Corporation, 1948– .

Greer, David, *Attorney at Law, Greer, Sibley & Dalton.* Term Member of the Corporation, 1945–56.

Griswold, Merrill, *Honorary Chairman of the Advisory Board, Massachusetts Investors Trust.* Member of the Corporation, 1936– ; Board of Trustees, 1945– ; Committee on Development, 1945– .

Gross, Boone, *President, The Gillette Company.* Member of the Corporation, 1956– .

Gryzmish, Reuben Bertram, *Chairman of the Board, Alles & Fisher, Inc.* Alumni Term Member of the Corporation, 1953–57.

Hagemann, H. Frederick, Jr., *President, State Street Bank and Trust Company.* Member of the Corporation, 1948– .

Hanf, Adolf Walter, *Manager of Wholesale Credit, Esso Standard Oil Company.* Term Member of the Corporation, 1955–57.

Hansen, George, *President, Conrad & Chandler, Inc.* Member of the Corporation, 1944– ; Board of Trustees, 1948–52, 1954– ; Committee on Development, 1948–52, 1955– .

Hansen, John William, *Secretary-Treasurer, Iselin-Jefferson Company, Inc.* Alumni Term Member of the Corporation, 1958– .

Harriman, Henry Ingraham, *formerly Vice Chairman of the Board, New England Power Association.* Member of the Corporation, 1936–50; Board of Trustees, 1937–47; Committee on Development, 1937–47. (Deceased)

Harvey, Carroll Sherlock, *President, Arthur C. Harvey Company.* Member of the Corporation, 1943–49.

Haufler, Robert C., *Division Engineer, Liberty Mutual Insurance Company.* Term Member of the Corporation, 1955–60.

Henderson, Ernest, *President, Sheraton Corporation of America.* Member of the Corporation, 1956– ; Board of Trustees,

200

1957–   ; Committee on Facilities, 1957–60; Executive Committee, 1960–   .

Herter, Christian Archibald, *formerly Governor, Commonwealth of Massachusetts, and formerly Secretary of State, United States of America.* Member of the Corporation, 1948–   .

Higgins, Chester William, *Assistant Vice President and Personnel Director, American Mutual Liability Insurance Company.* Term Member of the Corporation, 1959–60.

Hodges, Charles Edward, *President, American Mutual Liability Insurance Company.* Member of the Corporation, 1948–   .

Hodgkinson, Harold Daniel, *Chairman of the Board and Chief Executive Officer, Wm. Filene's Sons Company.* Member of the Corporation, 1945–   .

Hood, Harvey Perley, *President, H. P. Hood & Sons, Inc.* Member of the Corporation, 1944–   .

Hotchkin, William C., *formerly President, Hotchkin Company.* Member of the Corporation, 1944–45. (Deceased)

Hovey, Chandler, *Partner, Kidder, Peabody & Company.* Member of the Corporation, 1936–   ; Board of Trustees, 1936–   ; Executive Committee, 1936–38; Committee on Development, 1936–37, 1938–40; Committee on Facilities, 1943–   .

Howland, Weston, *Trustee and Director.* Member of the Corporation, 1941–47.

Hubbard, Howard Munson, *Industrialist; formerly President, Greenfield Tap and Die Company.* Member of the Corporation, 1936–   ; Board of Trustees, 1941–44.

Hutchinson, Maynard, *Treasurer, Loomis-Sayles & Company, Inc.* Member of the Corporation, 1939–52; Board of Trustees, 1939–52; Committee on Development, 1938–52; Executive Committee, 1941–43.

James, Raymond Winfield, *Production Manager, Photek, Inc.* Term Member of the Corporation, 1945–47.

Johns, Ray E., *General Secretary, Boston Young Men's Christian Association.* Member of the Corporation, 1946– ; Board of Trustees, 1946– ; Committee on Development, 1948– .

Johnson, Arthur Stoddard, *formerly Chairman of the Board, Boston Young Men's Christian Association.* Member of the Corporation, 1936–49; Board of Trustees, 1936–49; Executive Committee, 1936–41; Committee on Development, 1941–43, 1947–48; Committee on Facilities, 1943–47. (Deceased)

Johnson, Charles Berkley, *General Agent, John Hancock Mutual Life Insurance Company.* Member of the Corporation, 1943– .

Johnson, Robert Loring, *Vice President and Treasurer, Boston Manufacturers Mutual and Mutual Boiler & Machinery Insurance Companies.* Member of the Corporation, 1953– ; Board of Trustees, 1953– ; Committee on Funds and Investments, 1953– .

Jones, Henry Campbell, *President, Arkwright Mutual Insurance Company.* Term Member of the Corporation, 1937–39; Member of the Corporation, 1952– .

Kaplan, Jacob Joseph, *Attorney at Law, Nutter, McClennen & Fish.* Member of the Corporation, 1943–52.

Kelleher, Michael T., *formerly Vice President, Marsh & McLennan, Inc.* Member of the Corporation, 1946–58; Board of Trustees, 1947–58; Committee on Facilities, 1947–58. (Deceased)

Keller, Carl Tilden, *formerly Partner, Lybrand, Ross Bros. & Montgomery.* Member of the Corporation, 1936–37. (Deceased)

Kerr, Harry Hamilton, *formerly President, Boston Gear Works.* Member of the Corporation, 1942– ; Board of Trustees, 1945– ; Committee on Development, 1945– .

Kimbell, Arthur W., *Honorary Chairman of the Board, United-Carr Fastener Corporation.* Member of the Corporation, 1955– .

Appendix B

Knowles, Asa Smallidge, *President, Northeastern University.* Member of the Corporation, 1959– ; Board of Trustees, 1959– .

LaBelle, John William, *Assistant to the Executive Vice President, Foster-Grant Company, Inc.* Term Member of the Corporation, 1953–55.

Lahey, Frank Howard, *formerly Director, The Lahey Clinic.* Member of the Corporation, 1941–51. (Deceased)

Lamprey, Kenneth Walker, *Controller, The A. B. Sutherland Company.* Term Member of the Corporation, 1953–55.

Larner, Edward Atkins, *Chairman of the Board, American Employers' Insurance Company.* Member of the Corporation, 1948–57.

Lawrence, John Endicott, *Partner, James Lawrence and Company.* Member of the Corporation, 1948–56.

Lazarus, Maurice, *President and General Manager, Wm. Filene's Sons Company.* Member of the Corporation, 1959– .

Lee, Halfdan, *Chairman of the Board, Eastern Gas & Fuel Associates.* Member of the Corporation, 1936–48.

Light, Galen David, *formerly Secretary-Treasurer, Northeastern University.* Member of the Corporation, 1936– ; Board of Trustees, 1941–43.

Lowell, John, *Vice President and Director, Boston Safe Deposit and Trust Company.* Member of the Corporation, 1958– ; Board of Trustees, 1960– ; Committee on Funds and Investments, 1960– .

Lowell, Ralph, *Chairman of the Board, Boston Safe Deposit and Trust Company.* Member of the Corporation, 1950– .

Luther, Willard Blackinton, *Attorney at Law, Peabody, Arnold, Batchelder & Luther.* Member of the Corporation, 1949– .

Macomber, John Russell, *formerly Chairman of the Board, The First Boston Corporation.* Member of the Corporation, 1936–

48; Board of Trustees, 1936–48; Committee on Development, 1937–40. (Deceased)

MacMaster, Edward Abbott, *formerly Attorney at Law, MacMaster, Hunt & Nutter.* Member of the Corporation, 1936–61. (Deceased)

Madden, James Lester, *Vice President, Scott Paper Company.* Member of the Corporation, 1952–55.

Madsen, Robert Emanuel, *Manager, International Accounts, Mobil International Oil Company.* Alumni Term Member of the Corporation, 1960– .

Mallion, George Arthur, *Assistant Dean, Lincoln Institute, Northeastern University.* Term Member of the Corporation, 1941–43.

Mann, Harvard L., *Partner, Spark, Mann & Company.* Alumni Term Member of the Corporation, 1956–60.

Manning, Joseph Patrick, *formerly President, Joseph P. Manning Company.* Member of the Corporation, 1936–44. (Deceased)

Marshall, Albert Edward, *formerly Vice President, Heyden Chemical Corporation.* Member of the Corporation, 1941–49. (Deceased)

Martin, Lawrence Henry, *President, The National Shawmut Bank of Boston.* Member of the Corporation, 1953– ; Board of Trustees, 1955– ; Committee on Development, 1955–59; Executive Committee, 1959– ; Committee on Funds and Investments, 1959– , Chairman, 1959– ; Treasurer of the Corporation and the Board of Trustees, 1959– .

Mason, Harold Francis, *formerly President, Boston Wharf Company.* Member of the Corporation, 1937–54. (Deceased)

McCoombe, Charles Mathew, *New England District Manager, Allen-Bradley Company.* Alumni Term Member of the Corporation, 1956–60; Term Member of the Corporation, 1959–60.

McDevitt, Edward Joseph, *Partner, Patterson, Teele & Dennis.* Term Member of the Corporation, 1948–50; Alumni Term Member of the Corporation, 1953–57.

McElwain, James Franklin, *formerly Chairman of the Board, J. F. McElwain Company.* Member of the Corporation, 1939–58. (Deceased)

McLaughlin, Edward Francis, *Lieutenant Governor, Commonwealth of Massachusetts.* Term Member of the Corporation, 1954–55.

McLellan, Hugh Dean, *formerly Judge, United States District Court.* Member of the Corporation, 1936–53. (Deceased)

Meo, Dominic, Jr., *Vice President, Salem Oil & Grease Company.* Alumni Term Member of the Corporation, 1955–59.

Mitchell, Don G., *Vice Chairman, General Telephone & Electronics Corporation.* Member of the Corporation, 1954– .

Mitton, Edward R., *President, Jordan Marsh Company.* Member of the Corporation, 1947– .

Mock, Harold Adam, *Partner, Arthur Young & Company.* Alumni Term Member of the Corporation, 1953–57; Member of the Corporation, 1959– .

Moore, Irwin Likely, *Chairman of the Board, New England Electric System.* Member of the Corporation, 1943– .

Morgan, Fred Lester, *formerly President, Morgan Brothers Company.* Member of the Corporation, 1939–46. (Deceased)

Morton, James Augustus, *Vice President, Loomis, Sayles & Company, Inc.* Member of the Corporation, 1953– ; Board of Trustees, 1953– ; Committee on Funds and Investments, 1953– .

Mosher, Ira, *President and Chairman of the Board, Ira Mosher Associates, Inc.* Member of the Corporation, 1944–55.

Moultrop, Irving Edwin, *formerly Consulting Engineer.* Member of the Corporation, 1936–57; Board of Trustees, 1936–57; Committee on Development, 1936–43; Committee on Facilities, 1943–55. (Deceased)

Mugar, Stephen P., *President, Star Market Company.* Member of the Corporation, 1960– .

Mumford, George S., *Treasurer, Scott & Williams, Inc.* Member of the Corporation, 1948– .

Nathanson, Edward Abraham, *formerly Attorney at Law, Nathanson & Rudofsky.* Member of the Corporation, 1949–55. (Deceased)

Newton, Clarence Lucian, *formerly Attorney at Law, Newton, Brickett, Weston & Hill.* Member of the Corporation, 1936–45. (Deceased)

Newton, Harlan Page, *Manager, Claims Division, Boston Gas Company.* Term Member of the Corporation, 1951–53.

Nichols, William Hart, *Vice President and Treasurer, W. H. Nichols Company.* Member of the Corporation, 1956– .

Noonan, John Thomas, *Attorney at Law and Partner, Herrick, Smith, Donald, Farley & Ketchum.* Member of the Corporation, 1950– .

Norwich, Samuel, *President, J. W. Strieder Company.* Member of the Corporation, 1942–49.

O'Keeffe, Adrian F., *President, First National Stores, Inc.* Member of the Corporation, 1954– ; Board of Trustees, 1958– ; Committee on Facilities, 1958– .

Olmsted, George, Jr., *President, S. D. Warren Company.* Member of the Corporation, 1945– ; Board of Trustees, 1948–52; Committee on Development, 1948–50; Committee on Facilities, 1950–52.

Olsen, Olaf, *formerly Vice President, Old Colony Trust Company.* Member of the Corporation, 1936–46. (Deceased)

Orr, James Hunter, *President, Colonial Management Associates, Inc.* Member of the Corporation, 1959– .

Parker, Augustin Hamilton, Jr., *President, Old Colony Trust Company.* Member of the Corporation, 1939– ; Board of Trustees, 1939– ; Committee on Development, 1940–41, 1955– ; Committee on Facilities, 1945–55.

Appendix B

Parsons, Edward Snow, *Business Manager, Northeastern University*. Alumni Term Member of the Corporation, 1959–60; Member of the Corporation, 1960– .

Peary, Theodore Roosevelt, *Controller, Ludlow Manufacturing & Sales Company*. Term Member of the Corporation, 1951–53; Alumni Term Member of the Corporation, 1954–58.

Peters, Andrew James, *formerly Mayor, City of Boston*. Member of the Corporation, 1936–38. (Deceased)

Phinney, Edward Dana, *Vice President, International Telephone and Telegraph Corporation*. Member of the Corporation, 1947– .

Pierce, George Edwin, *formerly Senior Vice President, The National Shawmut Bank of Boston*. Member of the Corporation, 1936–48. (Deceased)

Pierce, Roger, *Chairman of the Board, The New England Trust Company*. Member of the Corporation, 1936–45.

Porosky, Matthew, *formerly President, Eagle Signal Corporation*. Member of the Corporation, 1936–48. (Deceased)

Pratt, Albert, *Partner, Paine, Webber, Jackson & Curtis*. Member of the Corporation, 1958– .

Pratt, Frederick Sanford, *F. S. Pratt & Son*. Member of the Corporation, 1936–58; Board of Trustees, 1939–58; Committee on Development, 1941–43, 1946–58; Committee on Facilities, 1943–46.

Preston, Roger, *formerly President, S. S. Pierce Company*. Member of the Corporation, 1941–54; Board of Trustees, 1942–54; Committee on Development, 1943–54. (Deceased)

Prout, Harry Wendell, *formerly Treasurer, Home Savings Bank*. Member of the Corporation, 1936–45. (Deceased)

Rabb, Sidney R., *Chairman of the Board, Stop and Shop, Inc.* Member of the Corporation, 1937–48.

Rand, Stuart Craig, *formerly Attorney at Law, Choate, Hall & Stewart*. Member of the Corporation, 1939–56; Board of

Trustees, 1939–56; Committee on Facilities, 1945–55. (Deceased)

Rand, William McNear, *President, Monsanto Chemical Company.* Member of the Corporation, 1942– ; Board of Trustees, 1951–53, 1954– ; Committee on Development, 1951–53; Committee on Facilities, 1954–58; Executive Committee, 1959– .

Rantoul, Neal, *formerly Partner, F. S. Moseley & Company.* Member of the Corporation, 1946–56. (Deceased)

Raye, William H., Jr., *Vice President, The First National Bank of Boston.* Member of the Corporation, 1955– .

Redmond, Kenneth H., *President, United Fruit Company.* Member of the Corporation, 1958– .

Richards, James Lorin, *formerly Financier and Industrialist.* Member of the Corporation, 1936–55; Board of Trustees, 1936–55; Committee on Funds and Investments, 1936–52; Committee on Development, 1936–54. (Deceased)

Richardson, Frank Lincoln, *Honorary Chairman of the Board, Newton-Waltham Bank and Trust Company.* Member of the Corporation, 1936– ; Board of Trustees, 1936– ; Executive Committee, 1936– , Chairman, 1954–55; Committee on Funds and Investments, 1936–41, Chairman, 1936–37; Committee on Development, 1936–46, Chairman, 1936–46; Vice Chairman of the Corporation and the Board of Trustees, 1936– .

Richdale, James C., *Vice President, Colonial Beacon Oil Company.* Member of the Corporation, 1945–55.

Richmond, Harold Bours, *Chairman of the Board, General Radio Company.* Member of the Corporation, 1943–60; Board of Trustees, 1944–60; Committee on Development, 1945–55; Committee on Facilities, 1955–60.

Riesman, Joseph G., *Trustee.* Member of the Corporation, 1959– .

Rittenhouse, Charles F., *formerly Senior Partner, Charles F.*

Appendix B

Rittenhouse & Co. Member of the Corporation, 1944–60; Board of Trustees, 1947–60; Committee on Facilities, 1947–60. (Deceased)

Robinson, Dwight P., Jr., *Chairman of the Board of Trustees, Massachusetts Investors Trust.* Member of the Corporation, 1952– ; Board of Trustees, 1954– ; Committee on Funds and Investments, 1954–58; Committee on Facilities, 1958– .

Robinson, John James, *President, New England Telephone and Telegraph Company.* Member of the Corporation, 1942–46.

Rogerson, Charles Milton, *formerly Attorney at Law.* Member of the Corporation, 1936–44; Board of Trustees, 1936–44; Committee on Funds and Investments, 1936–41; Committee on Facilities, 1943–44. (Deceased)

Rugg, Robert Billings, *formerly President, National Rockland Bank of Boston.* Member of the Corporation, 1936–46. (Deceased)

Saltonstall, Leverett, *United States Senator from Massachusetts; formerly Governor, Commonwealth of Massachusetts.* Member of the Corporation, 1936– ; Board of Trustees, 1937–51; Committee on Development, 1945–46, 1949–51; Committee on Facilities, 1946–49.

Sanders, Russell Maryland, *formerly Treasurer, H. M. Sanders Company.* Member of the Corporation, 1941–59. (Deceased)

Sanger, Sabin Pond, *formerly Trustee and Director.* Member of the Corporation, 1936–38; Board of Trustees, 1936–38. (Deceased)

Sayles, Ralph T., *formerly Vice President, Loomis-Sayles & Company, Inc.* Member of the Corporation, 1947–57. (Deceased)

Seiler, Andrew Sebastian, *formerly President, H. J. Seiler Company, Inc.* Member of the Corporation, 1942–54. (Deceased)

Shea, Albert Leroy, *Staff Production Manager, Campbell*

Soup Company. Alumni Term Member of the Corporation, 1955–59; Member of the Corporation, 1960– .

Simmers, Richard Walter, *formerly Partner, Scudder, Stevens & Clark.* Member of the Corporation, 1953–59; Board of Trustees, 1953–59; Committee on Funds and Investments, 1953–59. (Deceased)

Simonds, Gifford Kingsbury, Jr., *President, Simonds Saw and Steel Company.* Member of the Corporation, 1948– ; Board of Trustees, 1951–55; Committee on Development, 1951–55.

Slater, Robert Edward, *Senior Vice President, John Hancock Mutual Life Insurance Company.* Member of the Corporation, 1960– .

Smith, Farnham Wheeler, *President, Lincoln Management Corporation.* Alumni Term Member of the Corporation, 1954–58; Member of the Corporation, 1959– .

Smith, William Armstrong, *President, William Armstrong Smith Company, President, Reliance Chemical Companies of Kansas and of Richmond, California.* Alumni Term Member of the Corporation, 1958– .

Spang, Joseph Peter, Jr., *Director, The Gillette Company.* Member of the Corporation, 1945– .

Speare, Frank Palmer, *President Emeritus, Northeastern University.* Member of the Corporation, 1936–52; Board of Trustees, 1936–50; Committee on Funds and Investments, 1938–40; Committee on Facilities, 1943–47; Committee on Development, 1947–49. (Deceased)

Sprague, Robert Chapman, *Chairman of the Board and Treasurer, Sprague Electric Company.* Member of the Corporation, 1953– .

Stafford, Russell Henry, *Moderator, International Congregational Council; formerly Minister, Old South Church, Boston.* Member of the Corporation, 1936–45.

Steadman, Chester Chandler, *Attorney at Law, Steadman &*

Thomason. Alumni Term Member of the Corporation, 1957– .

Stearns, Russell Bangs, *Chairman of the Board, Colonial Stores, Incorporated.* Member of the Corporation, 1957– ; Board of Trustees, 1958– ; Committee on Facilities, 1958–60; Executive Committee, 1960– .

Steele, Francis Robert Carnegie, *formerly Senior Partner, Patterson, Teele & Dennis.* Member of the Corporation, 1936–55; Board of Trustees, 1936–55; Executive Committee, 1936–52. (Deceased)

Stetson, Charles, *formerly Attorney at Law, Warner, Stackpole, Stetson & Bradlee.* Member of the Corporation, 1936–1953; Board of Trustees, 1936–53; Committee on Development, 1936–43; Committee on Funds and Investments, 1936–52, Chairman, 1936–52; Executive Committee, 1943–53. (Deceased)

Stevens, Abbot, *formerly Vice President, J. P. Stevens & Co., Inc.* Member of the Corporation, 1951–58; Board of Trustees, 1954–57; Committee on Development, 1954–57. (Deceased)

Stevens, Raymond, *President, Arthur D. Little, Inc.* Member of the Corporation, 1958–60.

Stevenson, Earl Place, *Chairman of the Board, Arthur D. Little, Inc.* Member of the Corporation, 1939– ; Board of Trustees, 1939– ; Executive Committee, 1940–43, 1945– ; Committee on Facilities, 1943– , Chairman, 1944– .

Stewart, John Harold, *Partner, Arthur Young & Company.* Alumni Term Member of the Corporation, 1958– .

Stone, David B., *Partner, Hayden, Stone & Company.* Member of the Corporation, 1959– .

Stone, Robert Gregg, *Limited Partner, Hayden, Stone & Company.* Member of the Corporation, 1951– ; Board of Trustees, 1956– ; Committee on Facilities, 1956–60; Executive Committee, 1960– .

Storer, Robert Treat Paine, *President, The Storer Associates, Inc.* Member of the Corporation, 1936–   ; Board of Trustees, 1936–   ; Executive Committee, 1936–43; Committee on Facilities, 1943–57; Committee on Development, 1957–   .

Stuart, Frank Horace, *formerly President, T. Stuart & Son Company.* Member of the Corporation, 1936–54; Board of Trustees, 1937–54. (Deceased)

Studley, Robert Lee, *formerly with Studley & Emory.* Member of the Corporation, 1936–37; Board of Trustees, 1936–37; Committee on Development, 1936–37. (Deceased)

Supple, Edward Watson, *Vice President, The Merchants National Bank of Boston.* Member of the Corporation, 1936–47; Board of Trustees, 1937–45; Committee on Development, 1936–38; Executive Committee, 1939–40.

Tenney, Charles H. II, *Chairman of the Board, Brockton Taunton Gas Company.* Member of the Corporation, 1955–   .

Thompson, George C., *President, The Goudey Gum Company.* Term Member of the Corporation, 1957–58.

Thompson, Ralph E., *formerly President, Scott & Williams, Inc.* Member of the Corporation, 1942–52. (Deceased)

Thomson, Earl H., *Attorney at Law, Thomson and Thomson.* Alumni Term Member of the Corporation, 1953–57; Member of the Corporation, 1958–   ; Board of Trustees, 1960–   ; Committee on Facilities, 1960–   .

Todd, Nelson Barnard, *Vice President, United Shoe Machinery Corporation.* Alumni Term Member of the Corporation, 1955–58.

Toner, James Vincent, *formerly President, Boston Edison Company.* Member of the Corporation, 1942–51; Board of Trustees, 1943–51; Committee on Development, 1943–51. (Deceased)

Toulmin, John Edwin, *Vice Chairman of the Board, The First National Bank of Boston.* Member of the Corporation, 1936–40.

Traylor, Mahlon Edward, *formerly President, Massachusetts Distributors, Inc.* Member of the Corporation, 1940–42. (Deceased)

Tuckerman, Bayard, Jr., *Senior Partner, OBrion Russell & Co.* Member of the Corporation, 1937–41.

Tulloch, Douglass Franklin, *Department Superintendent, Boston Edison Company.* Term Member of the Corporation, 1947–49.

Tyler, Chaplin, *Management Consultant, E. I. duPont de Nemours & Company, Inc.* Alumni Term Member of the Corporation, 1956–60.

Vogel, Eugene Joseph, *Treasurer and Manager, Wes-Julian Construction Corporation.* Alumni Term Member of the Corporation, 1960– .

Wadsworth, Eliot, *formerly Trustee and Director.* Member of the Corporation. 1936–59. (Deceased)

Wakeman, Samuel, *General Manager, Quincy Yard, Bethlehem Steel Company.* Member of the Corporation, 1945– .

Walcott, Eustis, *Vice President, American Policyholders Insurance Company; Assistant Vice President and Special Services Manager, American Mutual Liability Insurance Company.* Member of the Corporation, 1940– .

Walter, Harold John, *Vice President, Amerace Corporation.* Member of the Corporation, 1949– .

Webster, Edwin Sibley, *formerly Chairman of the Board, Stone & Webster, Inc.* Member of the Corporation, 1936–50. (Deceased)

Webster, Edwin Sibley, Jr., *formerly Partner, Kidder, Peabody & Company.* Member of the Corporation, 1951–57. (Deceased)

Weeks, Edward A., *Editor, The Atlantic Monthly.* Member of the Corporation, 1950– .

Weeks, Sinclair, *Chairman of the Board, United-Carr Fastener*

Corporation; formerly Secretary of Commerce, United States of America. Member of the Corporation, 1939– .

White, William Crombie, *Vice President and Provost, Northeastern University.* Alumni Term Member of the Corporation, 1952–56; Member of the Corporation, 1956– .

Wilkins, Raymond Sanger, *Chief Justice, Supreme Judicial Court of Massachusetts.* Member of the Corporation, 1959– .

Williams, Roy Foster, *Honorary Vice President, Associated Industries of Massachusetts; President and Managing Director, Alden Research Foundation.* Member of the Corporation, 1953– .

Wilson, Carroll L., *Engineering Administrator.* Member of the Corporation, 1955– .

Wood, John W., *President, J. W. Wood Elastic Web Company.* Member of the Corporation, 1954– .

APPENDIX C

DIRECTORS AND DEANS OF MAJOR NORTHEASTERN SCHOOLS AND COLLEGES

School of Law

1907-1918—Frank Palmer Speare, Dean (Mr. Speare was Director from the establishment in 1898 of the Department of Law of the Evening Institute of the Boston YMCA)

1918-1920—Bruce W. Belmore, Executive Secretary

1920-1935—Everett A. Churchill, Dean

1935-1936—Sydney Kenneth Schofield, Acting Dean

1936-1945—Sydney Kenneth Schofield, Dean

1945-1947—Stuart M. Wright, Dean

1947-1953—Lowell S. Nicholson, Dean

1953-1955—Joseph G. Crane, Dean

Lincoln Institute

1904—Frank Palmer Speare, Supervisor of Polytechnic School (also conducted Evening Preparatory School courses)

1907-1909—Franklin T. Kurt, Dean, Evening Polytechnic School

1909-1913—Hercules W. Geromanos, Dean

1913-1917—Thomas E. Penard, Dean

1917-1919—Thomas E. Penard, Dean, Evening School of Engineering of Northeastern College

1919-1921—Carl S. Ell, Dean

1921-1923—Carl S. Ell, Dean, Evening Polytechnic School

1923-1924—Carl S. Ell, Director of the Engineering and Technical Schools

1924-1927—Thomas E. Penard, Associate Dean of the Evening
   Polytechnic School
1927-1935—James W. Lees, Dean, Lincoln Institute
1935-1945—James W. Lees, Dean, Lincoln Technical Institute
1945   Donald H. MacKenzie, Acting Dean
1946-1954—Donald H. MacKenzie, Dean
1954-   Donald H. MacKenzie, Dean, Lincoln Institute

School of Business

1907-1909—Orlando C. Mayer, Dean, School of Commerce and
   Finance
1909-1911—Shelby M. Harrison, Dean
1911-1912—Clarence B. Stoner, Dean
1912-1914—Frank Palmer Speare, Dean
1914-1915—Harry C. Bentley, Dean
1915-1916—Frank Palmer Speare, Dean
1916-1917—Mark A. Smith, Acting Dean
1917-1922—Dana S. Sylvester, Dean
1922-1923—Fred Miller, Dean
1923-1928—Carl D. Smith, Dean and Regional Director
1928-1935—Carl D. Smith, Dean, School of Business
1935-1944—Russell Whitney, Dean
1944-1945—Wilfred S. Lake, Acting Dean
1945-1960—Albert E. Everett, Dean

The Huntington School

1909-1911—Ernest P. Carr, Dean, Preparatory School (day and
   evening)
1911-1912—Ernest P. Carr, Dean, College Preparatory School
1912-1919—Ira A. Flinner, Superintendent of Day Schools (in
   1913 the Association Day School was named The Huntington School for Boys)
1919-1926—Ira A. Flinner, Headmaster of The Huntington
   School
1926-1944—Charles H. Sampson, Headmaster
1944-1945—James W. Lees, Headmaster

Appendix C

1945–1946—William G. Wilkinson, Acting Headmaster

1946– —William G. Wilkinson, Headmaster (in 1950 the direction of The Huntington School was transferred from Northeastern University to the Boston YMCA)

College of Engineering

1909–1912—Hercules W. Geromanos, Dean, Co-Operative Engineering Courses in the Polytechnic School (day) of the Evening Institute of the Boston YMCA

1912–1916—Hercules W. Geromanos, Dean, Co-Operative Engineering School of the Association Institute

1916–1917—Hercules W. Geromanos, Dean, Co-operative School of Engineering, Northeastern College

1917–1936—Carl S. Ell, Dean

1923–1936—Carl S. Ell, Director of the Engineering and Technical Schools (day and evening)

1936–1940—Carl S. Ell, Dean of the Day Division (including the College of Engineering)

1940–1943—William C. White, Director of the Day Colleges and Acting Dean of the College of Engineering

1943–1945—William C. White, Director of Day Colleges and Dean of the College of Engineering

1945–1953—William T. Alexander, Dean of the College of Engineering

1953–1954—Alfred J. Ferretti, Acting Dean

1954– —William T. Alexander, Dean

College of Business Administration

1922–1928—Turner F. Garner, Dean of the School of Business Administration

1928–1935—Carl S. Ell, Dean

1935–1939—Wilfred S. Lake, Dean of Instruction of the College of Business Administration

1939–1942—Asa S. Knowles, Dean

1942–1944—Robert Bruce, Acting Dean

1944– —Roger S. Hamilton, Dean

217

College of Liberal Arts

1935–1939—Wilfred S. Lake, Dean of Instruction
1939–   —Wilfred S. Lake, Dean

College of Education

1953–   —Lester S. Vander Werf, Dean

APPENDIX D

NORTHEASTERN BUILDINGS AND ROOMS DEDICATED TO PERSONS, AND CREATED BY INDIVIDUAL GIFTS

Buildings

In honor of—

Godfrey Lowell Cabot
Robert Gray Dodge
Carl Stephens Ell
James Lorin Richards

Areas in Buildings

The Chapel

In memory of Charles F. Bacon

Lobbies, Lounges, Reading Rooms

In memory of—

Lieut. Stafford Leighton Brown
George Henry Clifford
Edward J. Frost
Henry Clay Jackson
Richard Mitton
Abbot Stevens
Robert Lee Studley
Edwin S. Webster
Stuart Mead Wright

219

In honor of—
> Godfrey Lowell Cabot
> David Frank Edwards
> Sebastian S. Kresge

The gift of—
> Clara and Joseph Fabian Ford
> Lillian and Harry Hamilton Kerr

Classrooms, Laboratories, Offices, Conference Rooms

In memory of—
> Albert Farwell Bemis
> Magdalena M. Bohnenberger
> Robert J. Bottomly
> Lizzie J. Burgess
> James R. Connors '57
> Bernard W. Doyle
> Dominic Esposito '53
> Anna Glass
> Samuel Glass
> Charles Hayden
> Merrill R. Lovinger '50
> Ethel H. Lyons
> Everett Richard Prout
> James Walter Reading
> Samuel and Mary Robinson
> Dana S. Sylvester
> Harold Hamilton Wade
> Edwin Sibley Webster, Jr.
> Russell Whitney
> Gordon E. Wright '38

In honor of—
> Albert Ellsworth Everett '23

The gift of—
> Frank L. Richardson '09 and Mrs. Richardson
> Joseph G. Riesman '18
> Julius Charles Santis '21

APPENDIX E

HONORARY DEGREES

A chronological listing of honorary degrees conferred by Northeastern University, with designation of the position held by the recipient at the time of the award.

1931

Arthur Atwood Ballantine, Lawyer, Root, Clark, Buckner & Ballantine—Doctor of Laws

Harrison Prescott Eddy, President, Metcalf & Eddy—Doctor of Engineering

Edward Morgan Lewis, President of the University of New Hampshire—Doctor of Laws

Frank Palmer Speare, President of Northeastern University—Doctor of Laws

1932

Raymond George Bressler, President of Rhode Island State College—Doctor of Laws

Charles Rice Gow, President, Warren Brothers Company—Doctor of Engineering

James Lorin Richards, Chairman, Massachusetts Gas Co.; Chairman of the Board, Boston Consolidated Gas Company—Doctor of Laws

1933

Henry I. Harriman, Financier and Industrialist—Doctor of Laws

Henry Tilton Lummus, Judge, Supreme Judicial Court, Commonwealth of Massachusetts—Doctor of Laws

Paul Dwight Moody, President of Middlebury College—Doctor of Laws

1934

Frederic Lauriston Bullard, Journalist, Author, Editorial Writer of the Boston Herald—Doctor of Literature

Dexter Simpson Kimball, Dean of the College of Engineering, Cornell University—Doctor of Engineering

Payson Smith, Commissioner of Education, Commonwealth of Massachusetts—Doctor of Laws

1935

Carl Pullen Dennett, Industrialist, Financier, and President, National Economy League—Doctor of Laws

Charles Thomas Main, President, Charles T. Main, Inc.—Doctor of Engineering

Edward Fuller Miner, President, Edward F. Miner Building Company—Master of Arts

Leverett Saltonstall, Speaker, House of Representatives, Commonwealth of Massachusetts—Doctor of Laws

Harry Stanley Rogers, President of The Polytechnic Institute of Brooklyn—Doctor of Science

1936

Lloyd Cassel Douglas, Author, Lecturer, and Clergyman—Doctor of Literature

Andrey Abraham Potter, Dean of the Schools of Engineering, Purdue University—Doctor of Science

Edwin Sibley Webster, Vice Chairman of the Board, Stone & Webster, Inc.—Doctor of Laws

Clement Clarence Williams, President of Lehigh University—Doctor of Engineering

1937

Sanford Bates, Executive Director, Boys' Clubs of America; Former Penal Institutions Commissioner of the United States—Doctor of Laws

Appendix E

Harry Ellsworth Clifford, Former Dean of the Harvard School of Engineering—Doctor of Science

William Lincoln Smith, Professor of Electrical Engineering at Northeastern University—Doctor of Engineering

Clyde Everett Wildman, President of DePauw University—Doctor of Laws

1938

Calvin Francis Allen, Professor Emeritus, Massachusetts Institute of Technology and Consulting Engineer—Doctor of Engineering

Henry Styles Bridges, United States Senator from New Hampshire—Doctor of Laws

Thornton Waldo Burgess, Author—Doctor of Literature

Philip Curtis Nash, President of the University of the City of Toledo—Doctor of Laws

October, 1938 (Dedicatory Exercises)

Winthrop Williams Aldrich, Chairman of the Board of Directors of the Chase National Bank—Doctor of Laws

Karl Taylor Compton, President of the Massachusetts Institute of Technology—Doctor of Laws

Harvey Nathaniel Davis, President of Stevens Institute of Technology—Doctor of Science

Dugald Caleb Jackson, Professor of Electrical Engineering Emeritus at the Massachusetts Institute of Technology and honorary lecturer—Doctor of Engineering

Henry Cabot Lodge, Jr., United States Senator from Massachusetts—Doctor of Laws

Edward Augustus Weeks, Editor-in-chief of the *Atlantic Monthly*—Doctor of Literature

1940

Joseph Warren Barker, Dean of Faculty Engineering, Columbia University—Doctor of Science

Horace Tracy Cahill, Lieutenant Governor of the Commonwealth of Massachusetts—Doctor of Laws

223

Arthur Walter Dolan, Associate Justice, Supreme Court of Massachusetts—Doctor of Laws

Edward Leyburn Moreland, Dean of Engineering at the Massachusetts Institute of Technology—Doctor of Engineering

1941

Godfrey Lowell Cabot, President, Godfrey L. Cabot, Inc.—Doctor of Science

Leonard Carmichael, President of Tufts College—Doctor of Laws

Wat Tyler Cluverius, President of Worcester Polytechnic Institute—Doctor of Engineering

Harold Glenn Moulton, President of the Brookings Institution—Doctor of Laws

G. Bromley Oxnam, Bishop of the Methodist Church, Boston Area—Doctor of Literature

1942

Ralph E. Flanders, Industrialist and Engineer—Doctor of Engineering

Hu Shih, Author, Scholar, and Diplomat—Doctor of Laws

Joseph Crosby Lincoln, Author—Doctor of Literature

Channing Pollock, Dramatist, Essayist, and Lecturer—Doctor of Laws

Roy Andrew Seaton, Dean of the Division of Engineering, Kansas State College; Director, Engineering, Science, and Management Defense Training Program of the Federal Government—Doctor of Science

1943

George Russell Harrison, Dean of Science at the Massachusetts Institute of Technology—Doctor of Science

Randall Jacobs, Rear Admiral of the United States Navy—Doctor of Engineering

James J. Ronan, Associate Justice of the Supreme Judicial Court of Massachusetts—Doctor of Laws

Appendix E

Brehon Somervell, Lieutenant General of the United States Army—Doctor of Engineering

William Pearson Tolley, Chancellor of Syracuse University—Doctor of Laws

1944

Igor I. Sikorsky, Engineering Manager of the United Aircraft Corporation—Doctor of Science

Arthur T. Vanderbilt, Counselor at Law and Dean of the School of Law of New York University—Doctor of Laws

Julius Ernest Warren, Commissioner of Education for the Commonwealth of Massachusetts—Doctor of Laws

Thomas John Watson, President of the International Business Machines Corporation—Doctor of Laws

Charles Edward Wilson, Executive Vice-Chairman of the War Production Board—Doctor of Engineering

1945

Bradley Dewey, President, Dewey and Almy Company—Doctor of Science.

Chester Laurens Dawes, Associate Professor of Electrical Engineering at Harvard University—Doctor of Engineering

Harvey Dow Gibson, President and Chairman of the Board of Directors of the Manufacturers Trust Company—Doctor of Laws

Ira Mosher, President of the National Association of Manufacturers—Doctor of Laws

Kenneth Roberts, Author—Doctor of Literature

1946

Frederick Lewis Allen, Editor-in-chief of *Harper's Magazine*—Doctor of Literature

Cyrus S. Ching, Director, Industrial and Public Relations, U. S. Rubber Company—Doctor of Laws

Jerome Clarke Hunsaker, Head of the Departments of Mechanical and Aeronautical Engineering at the Massachusetts Institute of Technology—Doctor of Engineering

Origin and Development of Northeastern University

William McNear Rand, President, Monsanto Chemical Company—Doctor of Laws

Francis Trow Spaulding, President-elect of the University of the State of New York—Doctor of Laws

June, 1947

Richard Evelyn Byrd, Scientist and Explorer—Doctor of Science

J. Anton de Haas, Professor of International Relations at Harvard Graduate School of Business Administration—Doctor of Laws

Mark Antony DeWolfe Howe, Editor, Biographer, Historian—Doctor of Literature

Thomas Kilgore Sherwood, Dean of Engineering at the Massachusetts Institute of Technology—Doctor of Engineering

September, 1947

Eliot Wadsworth, Treasurer of the Carnegie Foundation for International Peace—Doctor of Laws

January, 1948

Christian A. Herter, Member of Congress from the 10th District of Massachusetts—Doctor of Laws

June, 1948

Sinclair Weeks, Chairman of the Board, Reed & Barton Corporation—Doctor of Laws

October, 1948 (Fiftieth Anniversary Convocation)

Mary Ellen Chase, Author, Professor of English Literature at Smith College—Doctor of Literature

James Bryant Conant, President of Harvard University—Doctor of Laws

Luis de Florez, Consulting Engineer and Inventor, Rear Admiral U.S.N.R.—Doctor of Engineering

Bernard DeVoto, Author and Editor—Doctor of Literature

Robert Gray Dodge, Lawyer, Chairman of the Northeastern University Corporation—Doctor of Laws

Appendix E

Edwin R. Gilliland, Professor of Chemical Engineering at the Massachusetts Institute of Technology—Doctor of Engineering

John Patrick Higgins, Chief Justice of the Supreme Court of Massachusetts—Doctor of Laws

Percy Lavon Julian, Director of Research and Manager of Fine Chemicals for The Glidden Co.—Doctor of Science

Clarence Belden Randall, Vice-President, Inland Steel Company—Doctor of Laws

Edmund Ware Sinnott, Director of the Sheffield Scientific School at Yale University—Doctor of Science

Joseph P. Spang, Jr., President, Gillette Safety Razor Company —Doctor of Laws

Thomas W. Swan, Judge of the United States Circuit Court of Appeals for the Second Circuit—Doctor of Laws

Raymond Walters, President of the University of Cincinnati— Doctor of Laws

1949

Earl Byron Babcock, Chief Chemist, Firestone Tire & Rubber Company—Doctor of Science

Richard Lyon Bowditch, President, C. H. Sprague & Son Company—Doctor of Laws

George Henry Clifford, President, Stone & Webster Service Corp.—Doctor of Laws

Robert Cutler, Old Colony Trust Company—Doctor of Laws

Esther Forbes, Author—Doctor of Literature

Albert Haertlein, Professor of Civil Engineering at Harvard University—Doctor of Engineering

James R. Killian, Jr., President of the Massachusetts Institute of Technology—Doctor of Laws

1950

Frank W. Abrams, Chairman of the Board, Standard Oil Company of New Jersey—Doctor of Engineering

Margaret Clapp, President of Wellesley College—Doctor of Laws

Frederick Joseph Dillon, Judge of the Probate Court, Suffolk County, Massachusetts—Doctor of Laws

Crawford Hallock Greenewalt, President, E. I. du Pont de Nemours and Company, Inc.—Doctor of Science

Ralph Lowell, President, Boston Safe Deposit and Trust Company—Doctor of Laws

John Phillips Marquand, Author—Doctor of Literature

1951

Donald Kirk David, Dean of the Harvard Graduate School of Business Administration—Doctor of Laws

Herbert Thomas Kalmus, President and General Manager, Technicolor Motion Picture Corporation—Doctor of Engineering

Harold R. Medina, Judge of the United States Court of Appeals for the Second Circuit—Doctor of Laws

Don G. Mitchell, President, Sylvania Electric Products, Inc.—Doctor of Laws

John Christian Warner, President of the Carnegie Institute of Technology—Doctor of Science

Thornton Niven Wilder, Author, Teacher, Scholar—Doctor of Literature

1952

Arthur Stanton Adams, President of the American Council on Education—Doctor of Laws

Van Wyck Brooks, Author and Critic—Doctor of Literature

Thomas Dudley Cabot, Executive Vice-President, Godfrey L. Cabot, Inc.—Doctor of Laws

William Crombie White, Director of Day Colleges at Northeastern University—Doctor of Engineering

Raymond Sanger Wilkins, Associate Justice of the Supreme Judicial Court of Massachusetts—Doctor of Laws

1953

Erwin Dain Canham, Editor of the *Christian Science Monitor*—Doctor of Literature

George Hansen, President, Chandler & Company—Doctor of Laws

Clarence Decatur Howe, Minister of Trade and Commerce in the Dominion of Canada—Doctor of Engineering

Alfred Jacobsen, President, Amerada Petroleum Corporation—Doctor of Laws

Charles Franklin Phillips, President of Bates College—Doctor of Laws

Stanley Elroy Qua, Chief Justice of the Supreme Judicial Court of Massachusetts—Doctor of Laws

Robert Chapman Sprague, Chairman of the Board, Sprague Electric Company—Doctor of Engineering

Alan Tower Waterman, Director of the National Science Foundation—Doctor of Science

1954

Harold Claude Case, President of Boston University—Doctor of Laws

Harold B. Gores, Superintendent of the Newton Public Schools —Doctor of Laws

Clifford F. Hood, President, United States Steel Corporation—Doctor of Engineering

John L. McCaffrey, President, International Harvester Company—Doctor of Laws

David Thompson Watson McCord, Officer of Harvard University—Doctor of Literature

John Harold Stewart, Partner in the firm of Stewart, Watts & Bollong—Doctor of Commercial Science

Walter Gordon Whitman, Head of the Department of Chemical Engineering at the Massachusetts Institute of Technology—Doctor of Science

1955

Arthur B. Bronwell, President of Worcester Polytechnic Institute—Doctor of Laws

Harlow Herbert Curtice, President, General Motors Corporation—Doctor of Commercial Science

Frank L. Flood, Partner, Metcalf & Eddy—Doctor of Engineering

Caryl Parker Haskins, President, Haskins Laboratories—Doctor of Science

Charles Newton Kimball, President, Midwest Research Institute—Doctor of Engineering

Nathan Marsh Pusey, President of Harvard University—Doctor of Laws

John V. Spalding, Justice, Supreme Judicial Court of Massachusetts—Doctor of Laws

1956

Chester M. Alter, Chancellor of the University of Denver—Doctor of Laws

Catherine Drinker Bowen, Author—Doctor of Literature

Albert Ellsworth Everett, Director of the Evening Division and Dean of the School of Business at Northeastern University—Doctor of Commercial Science

George Keith Funston, President, New York Stock Exchange—Doctor of Laws

Ivan A. Getting, Vice-President, Engineering and Research, Raytheon Manufacturing Company—Doctor of Science

John Fitzgerald Kennedy, United States Senator from Massachusetts—Doctor of Laws

John Anthony Volpe, Commissioner of Public Works, Commonwealth of Massachusetts—Doctor of Engineering

1957

John Lawrence Burns, President, Radio Corporation of America—Doctor of Business Administration

Bruce Catton, Editor and Historian—Doctor of Literature

Thomas Wade Herren, Commanding General, First United States Army—Doctor of Laws

Asa Smallidge Knowles, President of the University of Toledo—Doctor of Laws

Appendix E

Calvert Magruder, Chief Justice, United States Court of Appeals for the First District—Doctor of Laws

Julius Adams Stratton, Chancellor of the Massachusetts Institute of Technology—Doctor of Laws

Carl Raymond Woodward, President of the University of Rhode Island—Doctor of Laws

1958

Peter Popow Alexander, Chairman of the Board, Metal Hydrides, Inc.—Doctor of Science

Jean Paul Mather, President of the University of Massachusetts—Doctor of Laws

Perry Miller, Professor of American Literature at Harvard University—Doctor of Literature

Arthur Jenkins Pierce, Brigadier General, of the United States Air Force—Doctor of Laws

Henry Bradford Washburn, Jr.—Director of the Boston Museum of Science—Doctor of Science

Nils Yngve Wessell, President of Tufts University—Doctor of Laws

1959

Charles Francis Adams, President, Raytheon Company—Doctor of Business Administration

William Thurlow Alexander, Dean of the College of Engineering at Northeastern University—Doctor of Science

Carl Stephens Ell, President of Northeastern University—Doctor of Science in Education

Arthur Bartlett Homer, President and Chief Executive, Bethlehem Steel Corporation—Doctor of Business Administration

Edwin Herbert Land, President, Polaroid Corporation—Doctor of Science

John O. Pastore, United States Senator from Rhode Island—Doctor of Laws

Louise Hall Tharp, Author and Lecturer—Doctor of Literature

231

Origin and Development of Northeastern University

1960

Raymond Floyd Howes, Editor, *The Educational Record*—Doctor of Humane Letters

Walter Consuelo Langsam, President of the University of Cincinnati—Doctor of Science

Perry Townsend Rathbone, Director, Museum of Fine Arts, Boston—Doctor of Humane Letters

Abram Leon Sachar, President of Brandeis University—Doctor of Literature

Right Reverend Robert J. Sennott, Chancellor, Archdiocese of Boston—Doctor of Civil Law

William E. R. Sullivan, Brigadier General, United States Army; President, U.S. Army Chemical Corps Board—Doctor of Science.

BIBLIOGRAPHY

Catherine Drinker Bowen, *Yankee from Olympus*, Little, Brown and Company, Boston, 1944

James L. Bruce, *Filling in the Back Bay and the Charles River Development*, Proceedings of the Bostonian Society, January 16, 1940

James L. Bruce, *The Rogers Building and Huntington Hall*, Proceedings of the Bostonian Society, January 21, 1941

Everett A. Churchill, *History of Northeastern University 1896–1927*, Boston Young Men's Christian Association, Boston, 1927

Melvin T. Copeland, *And Mark an Era, the Story of the Harvard Business School*, Little, Brown and Company, Boston, 1958

Dialogues of Alfred North Whitehead, as recorded by Lucien Price, Little, Brown and Company, Boston, 1954

John S. Diekhoff, *The Domain of the Faculty in Our Expanding Colleges*, Harper & Brothers, New York, 1956

John P. Dyer, *Ivory Towers in the Market Place*, The Bobbs-Merrill Company, Inc., New York, 1956

Albert Bushnell Hart, Editor, *Commonwealth History of Massachusetts*, The States History Company, New York, 1930

M. A. DeWolfe Howe, *Boston, the Place and the People*, The Macmillan Company, New York, 1903

Frederick Johnson, *The Boylston Street Fishweir*, Phillips Academy, The Robert S. Peabody Foundation for Archaeology, Andover, Massachusetts, 1942

Bibliography

Albert P. Langtry, *Metropolitan Boston, A Modern History*, Lewis Historical Publishing Company, Inc., New York, 1929

Kenneth L. Mark, *Delayed by Fire, Being the Early History of Simmons College*, Privately Printed, Boston, 1945

Daniel L. Marsh and William H. Clark, *The Story of Massachusetts*, The American Historical Society, Inc., New York, 1938

Samuel Eliot Morrison, *Three Centuries of Harvard*, Harvard University Press, Cambridge, Massachusetts, 1946

M. M. Musselman, *Get a Horse!*, J. P. Lippincott Company, New York, 1950

Clyde W. Park, *Ambassador to Industry*, The Bobbs-Merrill Company, Inc., New York, 1943

A Record of the Streets, Alleys, Places, Etc. in the City of Boston, City of Boston, 1910

Richard E. Sprague, *Cooperative Education in the United States at the Undergraduate Level*, M.B.A. thesis, Northeastern University, 1955

Arthur Walworth, *Woodrow Wilson*, Longmans, Green and Co., New York, 1958

Dixon Wecter, *The Age of the Great Depression*, The Macmillan Company, New York, 1948

George F. Weston, Jr., *Boston Ways*, Beacon Press, Boston, 1957

Walter Muir Whitehill, *Boston A Topographical History*, The Belknap Press of Harvard University Press, Cambridge, Massachusetts, 1959

William B. Whiteside, *The Boston Y.M.C.A. and Community Need*, Association Press, New York, 1951